A FAITH FOR

A Faith for Living

by

A. S. MANEY

William Sessions Limited
York, England

ISBN 1 85072 112 2

Printed in 11 on 12 point Plantin Typeface
by William Sessions Limited
The Ebor Press
York, England

Contents

Introduction

In the twentieth-century there is a largely unsatisfied need for a rational and convincing faith which will be an inspiration and a guide for living. The expansion of human knowledge in the last 200 years has been such that it is now uniquely difficult to find a faith which is congruent with other known facts. H. P. Dixon, a fine but little known poet, expressed this well:

> The more I learn, the more I may.
> Truth that beckons walks away.
> Climbing mountains of the mind
> Shows how far the rivers wind.
>
> Futility cannot withstand
> The upward urge to that high land
> Where vast horizons man may face
> And lose himself in depths of space.

Belief was easier when knowledge was very limited and man's credulity more highly developed than his critical faculty. Primitive people had primitive religious beliefs which eventually gave place to five great faiths which have survived: Hinduism, Buddhism, Judaism, Christianity, and Islam. Of these Christianity has spread most widely and achieved the greatest influence. In the Western world it is the dominant faith and, if a faith for our time is to be sought, it must first be asked whether Christianity adequately and convincingly fills the need.

There are good reasons for supposing that Christianity achieved its position of eminence because of its inherent virtues; but there is another reason. For more than a thousand years it was, almost exclusively, the religion of Europe, and this is a fact of significance. From the end of the fifteenth century European civilisation began to draw ahead of all the other great civilisations. It became more progressive and dynamic than they in scholarship, industry, exploration, science, and military power. This development continued until the early twentieth century, by which time European civilisation was the dominant force in the world: a dominance fortified by the European occupation of the American continents.

Since the Christian religion was closely linked with European civilisation this reinforced its claim to superiority over other faiths. The claim was made with assurance and yet the number of practising adherents in most western countries has shrunk to a small minority of the population.

Christianity came into being in a society and an intellectual climate very different from our own, and creeds which were formulated between the third and fifth centuries A.D. are still the basis of its faith. Many hymns and liturgies which are used today include ideas which are foreign to modern minds, and dogmatic assertions are made in sermons which lack any reliable supporting evidence. Indeed large sections of the Church seem to be anti-intellectual and less liberal than they were fifty years ago.

Some church members continue in this situation by adopting an uncritical attitude or a willing suspension of disbelief. Others are beset by doubt and either discontinue church attendance or continue for social reasons and because they recognise that there is much good in Christianity to counterbalance that which is incredible.

In assessing any system of belief it is necessary to take an objective view, examine the available evidence and draw reasoned conclusions from it. That is, however, a difficult thing for us to do. The entire culture of the Western world has been so moulded and imbued by Christian creeds, myths, convictions, and practices that, not only our religion, but our art, literature, music, education, and ethical standards have been permeated and largely conditioned by Christianity. Even for a non-churchgoer objectivity is not easy; but if, from infancy, one has been reared in a Christian home and church the task is very difficult. The traditional beliefs have become part of the weft and warp of life and the attempt to examine them objectively and critically is liable to be hampered by an irrational sense of guilt. One comes only slowly to realise that there is more virtue in an honest search for truth than in an unexamined faith.

At the conclusion of the first millenium of the Christian era most of Europe had been evangelised under the aegis of the Roman church in the west and the Greek Orthodox church in the east. Both these churches were based on the historic creeds and were monolithic in theology and practice. With the exception of the Unitarians, the churches arising from the Reformation retained the historic creeds but rejected some of the sacerdotal views and practices of the Roman church. Though divided into many sects, Christianity continued to command the nominal allegiance of nearly all Europeans until the Age of Enlightenment in the seventeenth and eighteenth centuries when certain thinkers began to challenge its beliefs.

The phenomenal expansion of human knowledge which occurred in the nineteenth and twentieth centuries was accompanied by a decay in religious faith, particularly in countries where intellectual and scientific progress was most advanced. It is difficult to avoid the conclusion that there is a direct relation between the growth in knowledge, coupled with the spirit of scientific enquiry, and the decline in religious faith.

Most people today live on a purely practical basis and concern themselves with little beyond their daily affairs. More thoughtful folk, outside the churches, may feel the need of a faith which gives meaning and purpose to life but do not find it in the creeds and life of the Christian church. Even within the churches there are many who do not share the orthodox beliefs, but they enjoy the fellowship and feel the churches should be supported because they have a good moral influence.

The fact that the mainstream Christian churches still adhere to creeds established some 1,600 years ago stands in contrast to the great advances in other fields of human thought. This is not to suggest that no thinking or research has taken place in connexion with the Christian religion. It has. For example a great deal of Biblical research has been done in the last 200 years; yet few preachers display much awareness of what the scholars have to say, and even more rarely do they seem willing to modify their views in the light of that research and of other relevant advances in knowledge.

Because traditional Christianity has had such a pervasive influence on our culture it is important to know whether this is a valid faith in the light of present knowledge. If it is we ought to be able to explain it in terms which are convincing to the modern man. If it is not the question must be asked whether any other form of religious faith is tenable today.

The Bible which is the source of our knowledge of the origins of Christianity, comprises a large number of ancient writings which are very different from modern books and scholarly expertise is necessary if a proper assessment of their reliability is to be made. In these writings we find history mingled with legend, fiction, and incredible stories of the supernatural. Such books cannot be treated as the work of a careful modern historian. Many Christians seem willing to acknowledge that portions of the Old Testament cannot be regarded as accurate history but are less willing to take the same view of the New Testament.

In the following chapters are some commentaries on these books. The present writer is not an expert Biblical scholar and can only claim an honest attempt to base his comments on the findings of those who are. There are differences of opinion among them, but with regard to many important matters there is substantial agreement. Most scholarly books of Biblical studies make difficult reading for the layman and this may explain why the results of Biblical scholarship are not better known. The chapters which follow are cast in a simpler mould. In his book *An Old Man's Diary*, A. J. P. Taylor writes 'I try to follow the rule given to me by my tutor, G. N. Clarke, "say simple things to simple men". That is easy because I am a simple man myself'. In that spirit this book is written.

CHAPTER 1

The Old Testament

THE BIBLE OCCUPIES A UNIQUE place in the life of the English-speaking peoples to whom, in the magnificent translation known as the Authorised Version, it became the Book of books, supreme in their affection and reverence. Our everyday speech bears witness to this since many phrases from the Bible have passed into common currency and no other book is so often quoted. The secularism which is prevalent today is apt to make us forget that for some 400 years the Bible in English was read by countless numbers of English-speaking people. In bygone days many of them read no other book, and every Sunday they heard it read aloud in their churches. Children listened to its stories at home and at school. Men have loved it and quarrelled about it, and we have all, consciously or unconsciously come under its influence.

Yet it is not *our* book. The Bible was the work of a people far removed from us by time, race, geography, and mode of life, and it is inextricably bound up with their history. Therefore we can only have a proper appreciation of the book when we know something of the people who produced it.

The roots of our religious life are deeply embedded in the first part of the Bible, the Old Testament. This consists of 39 small books which cover a wide spectrum of literary forms. Here are myths, legends, folklore, history, tribal laws, genealogy, proverbs, poetry, drama, and prophetic writings. Some of this is of little interest to us today and some of it seems barbaric, as indeed it is, for these books trace the rise of an ancient people from barbarism.

Yet there is a great deal in the Old Testament which ranks with the noblest literature in any language. Above all, it is the work of a people with a genius for religion who alone of all ancient nations came to believe in one righteous God. This religion was vital to the life of ancient Israel and can only be understood in relation to the nation's history.

There are no reliable historical records concerning the origin of the Israelites, only legend and tradition, but it seems that, at some remote period they were in servitude in Egypt, whence they eventually escaped, and, in about 1200 B.C., invaded the land of Canaan (now known as Palestine or Israel). After years of fighting they conquered the land, and their form of government at this time was a tribal organisation controlled by judges (or leaders). This organisation came to an end with the consecration of Saul as king.

Saul was followed by David, Solomon, and Rehoboam, but the harsh rule of the last-named king caused the northern part of the kingdom to revolt and break away as a separate kingdom called Israel, whilst the southern kingdom was known as Judah. This occured in 937 B.C. During the period of the two kingdoms the great prophets were Elijah and Elisha. The word 'prophet' is to be understood as meaning an inspired teacher, revealer, or interpreter of God's will. In so far as the prophets foretold future events it was by an intelligent estimate of the probable consequences of current actions and circumstances.

In those far-off days the behaviour of the Jews, like that of their contemporaries, was often barbaric, and there was a constant tendency for them to fall into the paganism of the surrounding nations. Therefore the prophets were forever recalling them to faith in the true God (Jaweh) and his laws. The prophets frequently preceded their pronouncements with the words 'thus saith the Lord'. This should probably be understood as the expression of a conviction that the pronouncement was indeed God's will.

Amos, the first of the writing prophets, had much to say concerning the exploitation of the poor and prophesied that evil would come of it. Hosea, with tenderness and great sensitivity, deplored Israel's unfaithfulness and sought to persuade his people to return to the love of God.

The first Isaiah, who was responsible for a major part of the first 39 chapters of the book which bears his name, saw the evils of his time and laboured vainly with kings to avert the disasters which he foresaw. He was active in the latter half of the eighth century B.C. and was a majestic writer. Isaiah was followed, in Judah, by Jeremiah. The latter is often regarded as a pessimistic prophet, but he had his reasons. Israel had been conquered by the Assyrians in 722 B.C. and many of her people deported – never to be heard of again. It was clear that a similar fate threatened Judah and it was, in fact, conquered by Babylon. Between 597 and 586 B.C. a large and influential section of the population was taken into exile in Babylonia.

From this group of exiles there emerged one of the greatest of the Old Testament authors. His real name is not known, but scholars refer to him as Deutero-Isaiah, or the second Isaiah. The book of Isaiah, as it now stands, is clearly the work of at least three different authors: chapters 1-39 by the first Isaiah, with some additional material; chapters 40-55 by Deutero-Isaiah; and chapters 55-66 by some later author or authors.

The great poet of the exile gave to his people in their home-sickness and sorrow a message of comfort, hope, and faith in the love of God, and couched it in matchless language:

> Sing, O heavens, and be joyful, O earth;
> And break forth into singing, O mountains;
> For the Lord hath comforted his people
> And will have mercy upon his afflicted.

After 50 years in exile the Jews were allowed to return to Judah and, during the long and arduous task of rebuilding the temple and city, the great names were the prophets Haggai, Zecheriah, and Ezra, and the governor of Jerusalem, Nehemiah.

Following the conquest, in 332 B.C., by Alexander the Great, the country fell under the rule of his successors and under the influence of a Greek civilisation which was alien to Jewish habits of life and thought – especially in matters of religion.

This period saw the end of the Old Testament writings. Through many centuries of conflict and tribulation the best of the Jews had retained their unique faith in one God and a relatively high standard of ethical values. Their struggle to preserve the faith shines through the literature of the Old Testament. The Jews felt their religion and history were indissolubly joined, and their famous authors expressed this feeling in language of great beauty, passion, and nobility. It is a unique literature because of the centrality of God. Indeed the ancient Jews could not think of life or history except in relation to God, the Creator and Lord.

The alleged authorship of many books in the Old Testament must be treated with scepticism. It was not uncommon for ancient Jewish authors to write religious books and ascribe them to famous persons who had long been dead. Alternatively, if the author of a notable work was unknown, it would be popularly ascribed to some famous figure of the past.

The first five books of the Bible, which we know as the Pentateuch, and the Jews know as the Torah, are ascribed to Moses; but scholars are certain that he could not have written them. Professor R. N. Whybray considers it probable that these books are the work of a single author of the sixth century B.C. who used a great deal of existing material, written and folklore, supplemented by his own imagination.

Many of the psalms are ascribed to David but it is unlikely that he wrote any of them. The Song of Songs was entitled the Song of Solomon, yet he certainly did not write it; indeed it has nothing to do with religion but is clearly a love poem.

Almost the whole of the Old Testament was written in Hebrew; the only exceptions being small portions of the latest books to be written. These passages were in Aramaic, a language which was widely spoken in the Middle-East. Since the writing of the Old Testament covered a span of time probably exceeding that between Chaucer and the present day, it will be appreciated that the Hebrew language changed considerably during those centuries. This helps scholars to date the various books.

The Hebrew language, particularly in its early period, had a small vocabulary, few adjectives and adverbs, and no clearly defined tenses; but its words were vivid, direct, and sensuous. Like Anglo-Saxon, the words reflected the basic homely things of common life. The stories are told sparsely and simply, with no unnecessary detail; but they are told with power. Take, for example, the lament for Jonathan:

> How are the mighty fallen in the midst of battle!
> O Jonathan, thou wast slain in thy high places.
> I am distressed for thee my brother Jonathan;
> very pleasant hast thou been unto me;
> Thy love to me was wonderful,
> passing the love of women.
> How are the mighty fallen and the weapons of
> war perished!

The later age of Hebrew writing, roughly from the exile onwards, produced the finest poetry in the Old Testament. This is found in many of the psalms, in Deutero-Isaiah, in the magnificent dramatic poem of Job, and in parts of Proverbs, Ecclesiastes, and the Song of Songs.

A special feature of Hebrew poetry is known as parallelism. This has a variety of forms. In one mode each line of verse is divided into halves which balance each other. For example:

> Weeping may endure for a night; but joy cometh
> in the morning.

Another method is to have pairs of lines which balance each other:

> The Lord is my light and my salvation; whom shall I fear?
> The Lord is the strength of my life; of whom shall
> I be afraid?

This method of writing produces a fine rhythm which does not stand in need of rhyme or regular scansion. Most poetry cannot be satisfactorily translated into another language, but this Hebrew poetry is supremely translatable. The following passage from the Authorised Version of the Song of Songs was regarded by Sir Arthur Quiller-Couch as one of the finest in English literature.

> Set me as a seal upon thine heart,
> as a seal upon thine arm;
> For love is strong as death . . .
> Many waters cannot quench love,
> neither can the floods drown it.
> If a man would give all the substance of his house for love,
> It would be utterly contemned.

The Old Testament contains some of the world's greatest literature, notable both for its superb style and its contribution to religious thought. It was the product of a small nation living in a war-torn land between 3,000 and 2,150 years ago. If we ask whence came its nobility the answer must be that it came from Israel's passionate belief in God and his righteousness. The 90th psalm expresses this:

> Lord, thou hast been our dwelling place in all generations.
> Before the mountains were brought forth,
> Or ever thou hadst formed the earth and the world,
> Even from everlasting to everlasting, thou art God.
>
> So teach us to number our days,
> That we may apply our hearts unto wisdom.
>
> And let the beauty of the Lord our God be upon us;
> And establish thou the work of our hands upon us;
> Yea, the work of our hands establish thou it.

In the Old Testament there is evident a progressive development in the Hebraic idea of God. He who was originally regarded as exclusively the God of the Jews came to be regarded by Amos as the God also of the surrounding peoples. In Deutero-Isaiah and Job he was worshipped as the Lord of creation and the whole cosmos.

Not only does this book provide the ground which nurtered much of our own religion and culture, but the voices of its prophets still speak to us across the years, as in Micah's words:

> He hath shown thee, O man, what is good;
> And what doth the Lord require of thee,
> But to do justly, and to love mercy,
> And to walk humbly with thy God.

Of the Old Testament books Christians have regarded most highly the prophetic writings and the psalms. Though these are also treasured by the Jews, for them the first five books hold supremacy. They refer to these books as the 'Torah' since they enshrine the first principles of Jewish law. These books are the foundation documents of their faith and nation. Here are the accounts of the creation of the universe, the origins of the human race and the Jewish nation, the sufferings in Egypt and the deliverance therefrom under the leadership of Moses – the lawgiver of Israel. It is written in the Torah that God, through the mouth of Moses, promulgated laws to cover every aspect of religious and daily life and also, in some detail, ordained severe punishment for transgressors. Directions of extraordinary detail are given for the maintenance or recovery of ritual purity, and for religious ceremonies. Many of these ordinances must have had their origin in the need to maintain peace and discipline within the tribes, or the need to observe hygienic practices in a hot climate. But the laws came to have an overwhelming importance in the religious life of the Jews and attracted a vast amount of interpretation and commentary. So complex did the whole matter become that a body of people known as the Scribes came into being whose purpose it was to expound and interpret the Torah.

CHAPTER 2

The Gospels

The four Gospels constitute the most important part of the New Testament and have had a unique influence on Western civilisation. These writings, therefore, claim our serious interest.

Many generations of Christians considered the New Testament to be the very word of God and infallible. It was, therefore, considered to be impious to question its authority. This view was almost universal until, in the second half of the eighteenth century, a German scholar, Reimarus, set in train a critical study of the New Testament which has continued to this day. All important ancient books are rightly subjected to critical examination by scholars who endeavour to establish the validity of the texts, check their historical accuracy, and understand their significance in the light of what is known of the life and thought of the society in which the authors lived.

Clearly such investigations should be pursued in relation to the New Testament, otherwise we would have no assurance that we are dealing with anything other than myths. The Gospels, in particular, have attracted more scholarly examination than any other books and have done so for two reasons. Firstly, because they are central to Western religion and culture and, secondly, because Jesus came to be regarded as God incarnate. It was vital, therefore, to discover whether the Gospel accounts are reliable.

Throughout the nineteenth century a great deal of valuable research and criticism provided a better understanding of the New Testament, but there was a marked tendency on the part of various scholars to depict Jesus as the sort of man they, as modern Europeans, would like him to be. This mode of thought was torpedoed by Dr Albert Schweitzer in a famous book which bears the English title *The Quest of the Historical Jesus*. In that book he surveyed the New Testament research done from Reimarus to Wrede. He also expounded the view that Jesus was a first-century Jew who held apocalyptic convictions concerning an early end of the world, and his thought-world and cultural background were so far removed from ours that we could not expect to have any real understanding of his life and work.

For a long time after the publication of Schweitzer's book few authors attempted to write books on the historical Jesus, but scholarly work on the Gospels continued. Little by little knowledge of the subject expanded through new lines of enquiry and, occasionally, by archaeological discoveries and the finding of other ancient documents which widened our understanding of the society in which Jesus lived.

The sheer volume of research and scholarly study which has been devoted to the Gospels might lead one to suspect that the scholars were suffering from an obsessional neurosis. The fact is, however, that the documents themselves present such problems that it is difficult, and often impossible, to establish the facts. The difficulties arise from three main factors:

1. The Gospels provide inadequate accounts;
2. Those accounts differ considerably;
3. Near contemporary references to Jesus outside the New Testament are so sparse that they are virtually useless. Even within the New Testament canon there is very little information about the earthly Jesus, except in the Gospels.

We are left, therefore, with the four Gospels as virtually our only source of information concerning the founder of Christianity, so it is important to know what scholars can tell us about these books.

The authorship of the Gospels is uncertain and this is not surprising because, in the period when these books were written, authorship, particularly of Jewish religious books, was frequently not attributed to the true authors. Sometimes books were credited to a notable person, alive or dead, other than the real author. It is unlikely that any of the Gospel authors were eyewitnesses of the ministry of Jesus but they may have derived information, directly or indirectly, from people who were.

The Gospels were probably written between the years A.D. 60 and 110. That is to say from 30 to 80 years after the death of Jesus. The epistles were probably written from 20 to 85 years after his death.

The first three Gospels, Matthew, Mark, and Luke, are known as the Synoptic Gospels because they contain much common material which can be arranged in parallel columns of similar, but slightly varying, accounts of the same incidents or teaching. Nearly all scholars consider that Mark's Gospel is the earliest and that Matthew and Luke, in the compilation of their Gospels, used Mark and a lost collection of the sayings of Jesus which scholars refer to as 'Q' (*Quelle*, source). Each of the evangelists seems to have had, in addition, some other sources of information. The Gospel of John is very different from the other three. Though based on Judaism it was clearly influenced by Hellenic modes of thought, and attributes long speeches to Jesus which differ considerably from his manner of speech in the other Gospels.

It seems beyond doubt that the Gospels, written so long after the events they describe, were ultimately based on an oral tradition. Stories concerning the life, work, and teaching of Jesus must have circulated amongst the early Christians and been used for evangelisation and teaching. Oral transmission is notoriously inaccurate because memories are unreliable and people tend to alter what they have heard in order to make it more interesting, more dramatic, or more suited to the effect they wish to produce. It does not take much imagination to appreciate that the stories relating to Jesus may have been altered considerably by oral transmission over 30 to 80 years. It is fair to note, however, that memorisation played an important part in Jewish education of the period, so the oral transmission may have been better than we could otherwise expect.

It is not very likely that any of the Gospel authors compiled their work in Palestine. The great Jewish revolt of A.D. 66, culminating in the destruction of Jerusalem in A.D. 70, resulted in the massacre, enslavement, or dispersal of a large proportion of the Jewish population. Also Christianity does not seem to have attracted many Jews – its great success was in the gentile world. The authors, therefore, were likely to be living in a Graeco-Roman environment where the early Christian churches were thriving. It follows that their opinions would be influenced by the kind of faith which the gentile Christians had embraced and by the modes of thought prevalent in the pagan world around them.

The Gospels were clearly intended for the edification of the early churches. They are missionary propaganda and cannot be regarded as objective biographies of Jesus. Indeed scholars are agreed that it is not possible to construct such a biography from the information given in the Gospels. It has been estimated that if all that is reported in the Gospels concerning the ministry of Jesus were gathered together it would only occupy a period of three weeks. Not only is the information inadequate but much of the evidence is conflicting, and the order of events appears to have been arranged to suit the authors' style and purpose rather than to reflect the true chronology, if indeed the latter were known.

The Gospels and Epistles are deeply impregnated with the beliefs which the early Christians had come to hold *after* Jesus was dead. Within this context each evangelist presented a picture of Jesus as he saw him and as he wished others to see him. Each Gospel was slanted to this end. So Matthew, for example, sought to prove that Jesus was the fulfilment of Jewish prophesy, the true Messiah, and he used every possible device to accomplish this.

The four Gospels do not always agree in their presentation of the facts. Some differences are minor, such as one would expect to find in reports by different people, but some are substantial and a few examples will illustrate the point.

Matthew and Luke affirm that Jesus was born of a virgin. Their accounts differ and are accompanied by prophetic dreams, visions of angels, heavenly choirs, and a strange star. The story is not mentioned by Mark and John, neither did Paul refer to it. This is surprising, if such a remarkable event occurred. Matthew contradicts himself. He gives a detailed genealogy to prove that Jesus, through his father Joseph, was descended from King David, then tells us that Jesus was born of a virgin so could not have been Joseph's son. The story appears to be mythical and imported to support the claim that Jesus was divine.

The accounts of the calling of Andrew and Simon Peter in Matthew's and John's Gospels are quite different. Another interesting variation is found in the story of the fig tree which was condemned to bear no fruit: in Luke it is a parable but in Matthew and Mark it is recounted as a miracle.

The accounts relating to the resurrection and ascension in the four Gospels and in the Acts of the Apostles are so different that it can only be said that no reliable account exists.

Scholars have sought by various means to establish what is reliable in the Gospel narratives, and what is not. The problems presented by the documents themselves and the lack of corroborative evidence from other sources seem to reduce the critics, at times, to near despair. A distinguished Biblical scholar, in a letter to the present author wrote 'I am not sure that we know anything at all about what Jesus taught'. Dr John Bowden in *Jesus: The Unanswered Questions* puts it differently: 'There is a good deal that we probably know about Jesus; the trouble is that we can rarely, if ever, be sure precisely what it is'.

There are two other hindrances to our understanding of the life, work, and teaching of Jesus. Firstly the great cultural gap which lies between his time and ours. We delude ourselves if we imagine that we can enter into a full understanding of people who lived 1,900 years ago in a land and culture wholly different from our own. Their religion was still centred on the Temple and a multitude of regulations relating to cultic purity governed many aspects of daily life. They believed in one God but also in demons, angels, miraculous events, and magic. Between their era and ours there has been a vast growth in knowledge which has had a profound effect on almost every aspect of human thought. We can read translations of what these people wrote but we cannot be sure of knowing what the words meant to them. Perhaps it is only in the simplest aspects of our common humanity that we may come close to them as we read, for example, the stories of the Prodigal Son and the Good Samaritan. These reflect timeless experiences: a father's love for his son and the kindly acts of a thoroughly decent man.

Secondly, there are the problems of translation. In the book quoted above John Bowden writes:

> Translations from Semitic languages like Hebrew and Aramaic is particularly difficult, because the very structure of the language is so different from those to which we are accustomed. This means that even if one translates Hebrew or Aramaic literally, it is possible to give a misleading impression of what the speaker intends.

Bowden goes on to explain that the language we speak dictates the concepts we are able to form and the way in which we think. It follows, therefore, that when one reads words which were originally spoken in a language very different from that which is being read, though the words of the translation may be the nearest possible equivalent to the original, the concepts conveyed may be different.

Jesus almost certainly spoke in Aramaic. The authors of the Gospels wrote in Greek, and we read translations of their work in English. This double translation is bound to result in a degree of failure to reproduce faithfully the concepts which were originally expressed. John Bowden also points out that some translators have, at times, allowed their own theological opinions to influence their interpretation of the text and, in addition, he draws attention to the unreliability of 'modern' translations in idiomatic English 'in this way Jesus is "modernised" into saying things which he never did'.

The conclusion we must draw is that it is unwise to take particular texts from the Gospels and build great arguments upon them.

As we read the Gospels we must be conscious of their limitations and remember that they derive from an age, a culture, and a language very different from our own. We cannot reasonably accept everything we read as factual or as an expression of eternal truth. An effort has to be made to separate the wheat from the chaff, and the effort is worth making for in these small books there is a great deal of wheat. Though the nature of the evidence precludes certainty, it is fair to say that, in relation to some important aspects of the life and work of Jesus, we can claim a high degree of probability. This is considered in the following chapter.

CHAPTER 3

Jesus

There is no doubt that Jesus lived and there is a substantial measure of agreement amongst New Testament scholars concerning a number of important aspects of his life and teaching. These are:

1. His message concerning the Kingdom of God and the imminence of its realisation;
2. His ethical teaching;
3. His relationship with and attitude to his contemporaries;
4. The miracles;
5. The parables.

Jesus came into a Jewish society that was by no means uniform in its religious views. Orthodoxy came later, after the destruction of Jerusalem in A.D. 70. At the beginning of the first century there were many different sects or groups within Judaism. Some we know little of; others are better documented: Scribes, Pharisees, Sadducees, Zealots, and Essenes (the community at Qumran which produced the Dead Sea scrolls was probably an Essene sect). All these sects revered the Torah and the Temple, and cherished similar eschatological hopes for the final judgement and deliverance of Israel but they differed in their interpretations and emphases. The claim made by his followers that Jesus was the promised Messiah was not unique. The same claim had been made for others, and, in its very earliest days Christianity was probably regarded as just another sect within Judaism. The long-held belief that certain passages in the Old Testament specifically prophesised the coming of Jesus is an opinion which few scholars would accept today. That belief stems from the writers of the Gospels, particularly Matthew, who endeavoured to show that in Jesus the hopes and destiny of Israel were fulfilled.

Ancient Judaism had much to commend it: a belief in a righteous God, a moral code, and prophetic writings which expressed lofty thoughts and aspirations. But the commandments and rules of conduct laid down in the Torah had spawned, by exposition and commentary, a vast number of precepts which were regarded as essential to ritual purity. Many religious leaders had come to equate observance of these rules with holiness.

By the time of Jesus, the Jews had become fiercely nationalistic and cherished hopes of a messianic deliverance. This was a consequence of the fact that their country had been conquered by a succession of powerful enemies: Egyptians, Babylonians, Assyrians, Greeks, and Romans. The Jewish nation was one of competing religious sects, its culture threatened by the influence of Greek civilisation, and its people burning with hatred of the Roman power which ruled them. Into this maelstrom came a young Galilean with a mission and a message. His mission, to turn men's hearts to God; his message to proclaim the Kingdom of God.

The records give no personal description of Jesus and, as has been seen, they are inadequate and unreliable in many respects. Nevertheless it seems clear that he was a young man who had no privileged position or antecedents, was highly intelligent, and had an excellent knowledge of the Jewish religion. It is possible that Jesus was a trained rabbi and the Gospel accounts show that he was occasionally given the title. He taught with an authority which astonished all who heard him, was an eloquent speaker, and used marvellous parables which are remembered and treasured to this day. He showed great compassion for the poor, the sick, and the outcasts of society. He inspired devotion in his followers, carried conviction as a teacher and leader, and was probably a personality of great charm and magnetism.

Jesus spoke often of the Kingdom of God, indeed it occupied a central place in his teaching and preaching. There were two aspects to this: firstly, the kingdom that is to come and, secondly, the kingdom observable and working in contemporary life. In the first century both Judaism and Christianity cherished a belief that, at some time in the future, God's reign would be perfected on earth and, for the Jews, an important element in this hope was that their nation would be freed from its oppressors. Jesus apparently shared this belief in the future establishment of God's Kingdom and believed that he, and to a lesser extent, his disciples would have vital parts in that event. It would not come quietly, but dramatically, a terrible day of judgement:

So at the end of time the Son of Man will send his angels who will gather out of his kingdom every cause of sin, and all those who deeds are evil, these will be thrown into the blazing furnace, where there will be wailings and grinding of teeth. Then the righteous will shine like the sun in the kingdom of their Father. (Matthew 13. 40-43)

Portents will appear in sun and moon and stars. On earth nations will stand helpless, not knowing which way to turn . . . People will faint with terror at the thought of all that is coming upon the world . . . Then they will see the Son of Man coming in a cloud with power and glory. When all this begins to happen stand upright and hold your heads high because your liberation is near. (Luke 21. 25-28)

It seems that Jesus also believed that these awe-inspiring events would occur within the lifetime of some who listened to his words: 'In truth I tell you, there are some of those standing here who will not taste death before they have seen the Kingdom of God'. (Luke 9. 27).

These apocalyptic views seem to indicate that Jesus, a Jew of the first century, shared in substantial measure the opinions of his contemporaries. However, Jesus also spoke of the Kingdom of God in a quite different way, as being active and dynamic in the present:

But if it is by the Spirit of God that I drive out the devils, then be sure the Kingdom of God has already come upon you. (Matthew 12. 28)

You cannot tell by observation when the Kingdom of God comes . . . For the Kingdom of God is among you. (Luke 17. 21-22)

Scholars tell us that the dynamic character of the Hebrew expression for the Kingdom of God cannot be satisfactorily translated. Jesus appears to have felt himself to be God's chosen instrument for bringing the Kingdom on earth, so it was already present in his healing and teaching. Like his contemporaries he believed that Satan was the source of all evil power and illness was the result of demonic possession. Therefore his healing work was evidence of the power of the Kingdom of God ranged against the forces of evil; and God would prevail.

The ethical teaching of Jesus did not consist of a system of rules for living. It was not a revised edition of the Mosaic laws. Indeed he saw that a literal obedience to these laws had become a serious impediment to humane behaviour. He taught that there are two great essentials for righteousness and salvation: love of God and love of man. When asked which is the greatest commandment in the law he replied 'Love the Lord your God with all your heart, with all your soul, and with all your mind. That is the greatest commandment. The second is like it: love your neighbour as yourself'. These commandments are drawn from the Torah and provide a further example of Jesus's firm place in the Jewish tradition. For him the two commandments were inseperable, though many of his countrymen had not realised the fact. Yet only a generation before Jesus the Rabbi Hillel had said in reply to a question 'Whatever is hateful to you, do not do to your fellow-man. This is the whole Torah. The rest is commentary'.

So the statement made by Jesus was neither original nor unique. What was unique was the passion and eloquence with which he preached that the love of God and love of man were inseperable and one cannot sincerely hold to the first without practising the second. He raised this principle to new heights and illustrated it in memorable parables. Moreover he practised what he preached by over-riding the narrow dictates of the law when it would have obstructed an act of kindness such as healing a man on the Sabbath. He also demonstrated his sympathy for and fellowship with the outcasts of 'respectable' society. It is not too much to say that the light which Jesus threw on this principle for living was a landmark in human history. It stands as a challenge to the conscience of every man. It rings true and, when we are guided by it, life is transformed.

There are many kinds of love; the love of parent for child, of man and wife, of friend for friend, of a kindly person for those in need of help; and some languages have several words to express the different kinds of love. It is unfortunate that the English language has one word only and no satisfactory synonyms. 'Charity', 'kindness', and 'concern' are often used but do not adequately convey our meaning in many instances. The word 'love' has also been cheapened by its over-frequent use with a sexual connotation and in trivial 'pop' songs. When, therefore, we are charged to 'love our neighbour' the words might be taken to mean that we should have the same sort of affection for the people next door as we have for our family or for our dearest friends. This may well be impossible and it is not what the command means. It means that we should have a concern for, and be ready to offer kindness and help to, any folk who are in need or distress. Only on such a basis can human life be lived well and happily on this planet. Kagawa, a fine Japanese Christian, echoed the teaching of Jesus when he said 'Love is the law of life'.

Though the love commandment of Jesus is of fundamental value his recorded teaching is less explicit concerning its application to normal life. He was a wandering preacher who apparently believed that the existing world order would soon come to a cataclysmic end on judgement day, and he was passionately concerned to turn men's hearts to God whilst yet there was time. Having no settled occupation, no home, wife, or children, his ethic was intensely personal and he seems, at times, to have disregarded the responsibilities of people who lived a normal life. To a disciple who wished to go and bury his father Jesus said 'Follow me and leave the dead to bury their dead'. In Luke 14. 26 he is reported as saying 'If anyone comes to me and does not hate his father and mother, wife and children, brothers and sisters, even his own life, he cannot be a disciple of mine'. The injunction in the Sermon on the Mount 'I tell you not to be anxious about food and drink to keep you alive and about clothes to cover your body' may have been declamatory to make a point, but is certainly advice which many poor folk could not take.

It has to be said that no human society can survive on a basis of improvidence and poverty. We cannot help our neighbours if we have nothing with which to help them. Jesus does not seem to have paid much attention to the social problems of his time. Perhaps the greatest social evil in the ancient world was the universal institution of slavery – surely one of the most grievous wrongs that can be inflicted by man on man; yet Jesus had nothing to say about that or about some other major social problems. True it is that if the love commandment is properly understood and implemented it will go far to solve most social problems. Yet people need help to see that. High principles are of little use if we cannot see how to apply them, and people need to be roused to action, as most social reformers have known.

The problems faced by the human race are numerous and complex. They call for a thorough investigation of the facts and intelligence in seeking a solution. Love is essential but it is not enough: we also need wisdom. These are aspects which are not found in the Gospels, indeed there are suggestions of a distaste for knowledge and wisdom: 'I thank you, Father, Lord of heaven and earth, for hiding these things from the learned and wise and revealing them to the simple'. We shall not solve the problems of our time without a deep concern for our fellow men and women, neither shall we solve them without knowledge and wisdom. We need the learned and wise if we are to establish a good community on this earth.

Jesus showed that a slavish obedience to the Judaic laws had become, for many, an obsession which inhibited the exercise of kindliness and charity. He taught that the pre-requisite for salvation is a simple acceptance of the love and forgiveness which God offers, and a sincere turning around to live in his way. Professor Dodd has said that this is the real meaning of the word which has been translated as 'repentance'. The publican who prayed sincerely was acceptable to God even though he was a social outcast; the Pharisee who was self-satisfied and smug because of his adherence to the law was not acceptable. Jesus lost few opportunities to commend sincerity and condemn hypocrisy.

Though Jesus did not oppose the Judaic laws, he clearly favoured a much less stringent application of them than did other contemporary religious leaders. Yet his call for submission to the will of God was so absolute that it might be felt to be more demanding than a strict obedience to the law. This, however, was balanced by his teaching concerning God's limitless love and forgiveness which are available to all who sincerely turn to him – they do not have to deserve it.

The accounts of the miracles which Jesus is said to have performed raise doubts for many thoughtful people. In the twentieth century knowledge of the natural world is so far in advance of the first century that some of these accounts now seem incredible. Magic has been relegated to fairy stories. It is probable that some of the accounts are myths deriving from the belief that Jesus was divine. Common attributes of divinity in the first century (and there were many divinities) were virgin birth, the ability to perform paranormal acts, and coming back to life after death. Such ideas were rife in the Graeco-Roman world into which the Christian sect rapidly moved. Even in Judaism there was a general belief in the miraculous and in supernatural beings. It was almost inevitable that accounts of miracles would be drawn into the tradition relating to a charismatic religious leader.

However, the healing miracles of Jesus occupy such a prominent place in the Gospel stories that they are likely to have a foundation in fact. Confirmation of this is seen in the attitude of those who opposed him: they did not deny that he performed miracles but accused him of doing it by the power of Satan. Both Jesus and his enemies believed that illness was caused by demonic possession and he countered their accusation by asking 'how can Satan cast out Satan?' If Jesus had been merely a deviant religious teacher the threat to the Jewish establishment would not have been great, but when his claims were reinforced by remarkable deeds they became serious and were recognised as such.

We now know that much illness is of psychosomatic origin. There is no doubt that Jesus was a man of immense charisma and faith, also the people with whom he was dealing were, by present standards, simple and unsophisticated. It is likely that such folk, if suffering from psychosomatic illness, would be restored to health because they really believed that Jesus could heal them. Because he believed God would heal them, they believed it too, and they were healed. Some of the ills that were healed may not have had a psychosomatic origin. We cannot recover the facts, and even in the present state of medical knowledge there is still much to learn.

The stories of miracles which are not concerned with healing but seem contrary to natural law may properly be regarded with greater scepticism. These are such matters as walking on the water, turning water into wine, bringing the dead back to life, and feeding 5,000 people with five loaves and two fish. Critical examination of such accounts show that the miracle stories may have originated or been exaggerated in the course of tradition. In some instances what was originally a parable may have been changed into an event. As mentioned in the previous chapter, the story of the fig tree which bore no fruit is a parable in Luke 13. 6-9 and in Matthew 21. 18-21 it has become a miracle.

Many of the stories relating to the behaviour of Jesus towards his contemporaries are likely to be historically reliable. His humane attitude to the outcasts of Jewish society was remarkable. These were such folk as Samaritans (heretics), gentiles, harlots, and publicans (tax-gatherers working for the Romans). Whilst not condoning their faults he was ready to enter into fellowship with them and made it clear that God's forgiveness and acceptance were open to them also. When criticised for this by the scribes and pharisees he responded both with defence and attack, and employed a number of delightful parables in making his point.

Jesus appears to have behaved differently towards his critics and opponents; in these relations there is little evidence of calmness or charity. In Matthew 23. 13-33 there is reported a violent condemnation containing such phrases as 'Lawers and Pharisees, hypocrites . . . blind guides . . . when you have won him [a convert] you make him twice as fit for hell as you are yourselves . . . blind fools . . . you are like tombs covered in whitewash but inside you are brimful of hypocrisy and crime . . . you snakes, you viper's brood, how can you escape being condemned to hell?' There are other similar passages, also a number of instances where Jesus promises eternal punishment for those whose righteousness falls short of his demands. Some of these are to be found in parables, but the meaning is plain: eternal torture and the fires of hell await the unrighteous. (See Matthew 18. 34-35; 22. 13-14; Luke 10. 11-12; 17. 29-30; 19. 27).

Evil must be opposed firmly and its probable consequences plainly stated but in many of these passages there is an odour of fanaticism and cruelty which ill accords with the teaching 'love your enemies and pray for your persecutors . . . pass no judgement and you will not be judged'. We do not know how accurately these violent passages in the Gospels reflect the actual words of Jesus and there is some evidence that the violence of the language in Matthew's Gospel comes from the evangelist and not from Jesus. With regard to the criticisms which he is alleged to have directed against the Scribes and Pharisees, there are reasons why the reported words may have been more pungent than the original. The early Christians must have felt less than charitable towards the Jewish religious establishment which encompassed the execution of Jesus and, for other reasons, the gap between Judaism and Christianity was widening at the time when the Gospels were written. Also the war between the Jews and Rome which concluded in A.D. 70 left a strong legacy of animosity between Rome and the Jews. Since the Christians, mainly of Gentile origin, sought tolerance from Rome, they would desire to distance themselves from the Jews and this may have led the authors of the Gospels to exaggerate criticism of the Jewish leaders. Nevertheless, these condemnations may have had a basis in what Jesus actually said. If this be so it implies something less than perfection.

Who or what did Jesus consider himself to be? This is one of the most important questions arising from the Gospels and one of the most difficult to answer. It is generally agreed by scholars that he made no specific claim to be the Messiah. The two passages where he appears to imply this (Matthew 23. 10 and Mark 9. 41) are regarded as later additions. Nor did he specifically reject the title. The Jewish Messianic expectation looked for a leader who would overthrow Israel's enemies and usher in the Kingdom of God. With the first of these hopes Jesus could not identify himself, but with the second he could. It was clearly difficult, therefore, for him to accept or reject the title. Nevertheless, Christians, at a later date, referred to him as the Messiah, using the Greek form 'the Christ' with a rather different connotation.

Jesus frequently used the term 'Son of Man' but it is far from clear what he meant. Geza Vermes, a distinguished Jewish scholar, states that, in literature of the time when Jesus lived, the term was not used as a title but meant 'I' or 'man'. The book of Daniel mentions a heavenly figure as a 'son of man' and it is possible that, on some occasions, Jesus was referring to such a one, not himself. Very rarely he is reported as using the words 'the Son' with reference to himself, but some scholars regard the words as inauthentic.

No Jew devoted to his faith would have claimed to be God incarnate. Such a claim would have been the ultimate blasphemy. There is no evidence that Jesus made the claim and even his enemies never accused him of doing so. When a man asked him 'Good teacher, what must I do to win eternal life?' Jesus replied 'Why do you call me good? No one is good save God alone'. (Mark 10. 17-18). In John 14. 28 he said 'If you loved me you would be glad that I am going to the Father; for the Father is greater than I am'.

When a scribe asked Jesus which was the first of all the commandments, he replied 'The first is "Hear, O Israel: the Lord our God is the one Lord, and you must love the Lord your God with all your heart, with all your soul, with all your mind, and with all your strength"'. In his book *Jesus: the Evidence* Ian Wilson comments on this passage:

> Here was nothing about a call for belief in himself as mankind's saviour, nothing about a new religion that he wanted instituted in his name. Instead, in choosing this commandment, Jesus was affirming in the most emphatic way possible that the Jewish faith was the absolute bedrock of his belief. The quotation is not just a passage from Deuteronomy, it is the great *Shema Israel* (Listen Israel) the confession of faith which every practising Jew recites morning and evening every day of his life.

We have no clear indication of what Jesus thought himself to be. Some people regarded him as a prophet and he may have been of the same opinion. Certainly he felt close to God, was sure he had been commissioned by God, and that he was able to communicate God's will to men. He referred to God as his Father but also frequently spoke of 'our' Father and 'your' Father, so it is hard to see how any claim was made for a unique sonship. There is no reliable evidence of a claim to divinity, only an enigma.

There is a considerable degree of agreement that the recorded pronouncements of Jesus concerning his approaching death and resurrection were moulded to conform with the views which had come to prevail in the early church. Also it is thought that the prediction that Jesus would be raised after three days was a later addition.

Meals with the family or with close friends had great significance for the Jews, particularly on special occasions such as the Passover meal. Such an occasion was the last supper which Jesus had with his disciples. It had no more sacramental character than the earlier meals he had shared with them, but was solemnised by the foreboding of the tragedy to come. We cannot be sure of what Jesus said at that last supper, the Gospel accounts differ. Some authorities take the view that Jesus had no thought of establishing a sacramental rite, but linked with the familiar blessing an announcement and interpretation of his imminent death. He would be familiar with the passages in the book of Isaiah concerning the suffering servant of the Lord and may have thought of his coming death in those terms. He seems to have implied that his death would seal a covenant. He may have meant that God covenanted with men to forgive the sins of all who sincerely turned to him. It is unlikely that he intended what was later propounded as the doctrine of atonement: that God required the death of Jesus to purchase forgiveness of other men's sins. This presupposes an immoral God. If such a doctrine is combined with belief in the divinity of Jesus it is seen to be even more absurd: God demanding his own death to atone for mankind's sins against himself.

The arrest, trial, and crucifixion of Jesus followed closely upon the last supper but the events which ensued are enigmatic. The stories in the Gospels are confused, contradictory, and cannot satisfactorily be reconciled. The accounts differ as to who found the empty tomb and what took place when they found it. With regard to the appearances of Jesus to the disciples after his death, Matthew says this occurred on a mountain in Galilee. Mark states that Jesus appeared first to two followers as they walked in the country, then to the eleven as they dined, presumably in Jerusalem. Luke agrees substantially with Mark but adds additional detail. John records three appearances: two in Jerusalem and one in Galilee – though not on a mountain, as Matthew said, but by the lake. Matthew makes no mention of an ascension; Mark tells us that this took place immediately after Jesus's appearance to the disciples in Jerusalem. John makes no reference to an ascension and the Acts of the Apostles says it took place after forty days when 'he was lifted up and a cloud received him from their sight'.

The matter is further complicated by the fact that the last twelve verses of Mark are almost certainly not part of the original Gospel but a later attempt to provide an ending to a mutilated document. These are passages which recount the events succeeding the resurrection. This material does not appear in some of the ancient documents and must be regarded as unreliable.

It may be that we can assess the nature of these records by their improbable accounts of the signs and wonders which are alleged to have taken place when Jesus died. There was an eclipse of the sun, the curtain of the temple was torn in two, there was an earthquake, the rocks split, graves opened and many came out of the graves and walked in Jerusalem. Later another earthquake moved the stone from the tomb and an angel came down from heaven and sat on it. Such accounts convey a sense of fantasy rather than fact.

We know that when a person has died, when his heart has stopped beating for a certain period, there is no possibility of his coming to life again. In order to carry conviction to the contrary the evidence would have to be of a very high order and the evidence in the Gospels is far from that.

Nevertheless the disciples appear to have been convinced that Jesus had, in some way, been restored to life. It may be that they first conceived of a spiritual resurrection which was later transformed into belief in a physical resurrection – a belief which was consistent with some contemporary Jewish thinking. It must be noted also that similar phenomena were in those days attributed to nature gods, important rulers, heroes, and philosophers. Though the reports concerning the appearances of Jesus after death do not tally, it seems likely that some kind of experience gave rise to the reports. Were they visions, delusions, or (as some have suggested) the result of post-hypnotic suggestion? We cannot understand the psychology of people so far removed from us in time and culture, but of this we may be sure that the personality of Jesus must have had a tremendous impact on his disciples. They may have believed that God would not let him die and have had visionary experiences to confirm that. If a few had such an experience a chain reaction would be likely, so giving rise to a new theology.

CHAPTER 4

Christianity

BECAUSE JESUS EXPECTED THE DAY of Judgement and the establishment of God's kingdom within the lifetime of some of his followers, he probably saw no need to found an organisation such as that which we know as the Church. According to the Revised English Bible the word 'church' occurs only once in the Gospels: 'You are Peter, the rock; and on this rock I will build my church'. (Matthew 16. 18). This isolated reference may be inauthentic. No such institution as a 'church' existed at that time. The word which has been so translated probably meant the eschatological community of Israel; also it was not Peter but James, the brother of Jesus, who became head of the Christian community in Jerusalem.

The little we know of that first Christian community is to be found in the Acts of the Apostles. In the fourth chapter there is an appealing glimpse of this modest group seeking to mould their common life in accordance with the teaching of Jesus:

> The whole body of believers was united in heart and soul. Not a man of them claimed any of his possessions as his own, but everything was held in common . . . they had never a needy person among them, because all who had property in land or houses sold it, brought the proceeds of the sale, and laid the money at the feet of the apostles; it was then distributed to any who stood in need.

That was not a way of life which could be sustained in the long term but it was an understandable expedient for a community which expected an early end of the current world order. A rather different note was struck by Peter's first speech in public, and this was a pattern which was followed in much subsequent Christian preaching:

Men of Israel, listen to me: I speak of Jesus of Nazareth, a man singled out by God and made known to you through miracles, portents, and signs, which God worked among you through him . . . you used heathen men to crucify and kill him. But God raised him to life again.

There is nothing in that speech, and little in the whole book of Acts, concerning the teaching of Jesus. The emphasis was on his person, not yet God, but the Messiah, the Christ; to believe in whom is the prerequisite for salvation. This affirmation is not supported by reason but by 'miracles, portents, and signs'. There can be little doubt that the early Christians communicated as much as they could remember of the teaching of Jesus, but they seem to have placed greater emphasis on his position in the divine hierarchy and they apparently felt the need to support this with stories of miracles and wonders. Such stories of miraculous deeds performed in the name of Jesus are numerous in the book of Acts and strain credulity to the limit.

Apparently in the very early days of the Christian community there were no clearly developed doctrines concerning Christ or atonement, no organised church, and no priests: just apostles, elders, and teachers. There are references to meals where there was breaking of bread and gospel teaching, but such meals were probably in the Jewish tradition and are unlikely to have had the sacrificial/sacerdotal significance of the eucharist of later years.

Information concerning the real life of the early Church is sparse in the New Testament and little is known from other sources. It seems that, of those leaders who are mentioned, Paul was the most able, dynamic, and articulate. Indeed he has been regarded by some as the real founder of Christianity as a separate religion. This overstates the case, but Paul certainly had considerable influence in modifying the gospel. Jesus was a Galilean Jew, probably from a peasant background. Paul was also a Jew, but from a sophisticated Greek city, and he was a Roman citizen. It was inevitable that there should be some divergence of view. The main thrust of the teaching of Jesus was concerned with the fatherhood and the kingdom of God, and love toward men and women. Paul preached Christ, crucified and risen, and justification by faith in him. This was a further step along the road towards emphasising the person of Jesus rather than his message.

Though Paul was active in taking the gospel to the Gentiles he was not alone in that. It was not he who took the gospel to Egypt and Rome. There were probably many Christians who travelled in the Empire spreading the good news and it seems that the Christian message was disseminated fairly rapidly throughout the civilisation which surrounded the Mediterranean Sea. This had considerable consequences for Christian theology, practice, and church organisation.

The attribution of divinity to Jesus was accomplished by degrees. At an early stage Christians referred to him as Christ and Lord. 'Christ' is derived from the Greek word for Messiah, but it came to have a meaning for Christians which was rather different from that which Jews attached to the word. John's Gospel was probably written in the closing years of the first century and influenced, to some degree, by Greek philosophy. Its opening passages are very different from anything in the Synoptic Gospels and from Palestinian Judaism:

> When all things began, the Word already was. The Word dwelt with God, and what God was, the Word was. The Word, then, was with God at the beginning, and through him all things came to be . . . the Word became flesh; he came to dwell among us, and we beheld his glory, such glory as befits the Father's only Son, full of grace and truth.

Here the author is affirming that Jesus existed from the beginning of time and is the only Son of God. This is virtually a claim for full divinity. Such a claim would have been considered to be blasphemy by the Jews but would have presented no difficulty to the Gentiles. Gods and goddesses were numerous in their world and divinity was frequently attributed to emperors and other famous people. By the early fourth century the overwhelming majority of Christians was of Gentile origin, so it should come as no surprise that a claim to the full divinity of Jesus was incorporated into the official creed of the Church in A.D. 325.

Christian converts must have been influenced by the pagan culture of the society in which they lived. First-generation Christians would have held pagan beliefs before their conversion and are unlikely to have been able to free themselves entirely from old habits of thought. Undoubtedly primitive Christianity was permeated by what the late Bishop Barnes referred to as 'the ancestral sacramental paganism of the Mediterranean peoples'. Priests soon replaced lay elders as leaders in the Church, and took to shaving their heads like the priests of the Egyptians. Goddesses had an important place in pagan religion and Christianity had no goddess, but the mother of Jesus was elevated to a semi-divine position: first came the story of the miraculous birth of her son; in A.D. 431 the Council of Ephesus gave her the title *Theotokus*, meaning God-bearing or Mother of God. She became an object of adoration, so in 1854 it became Catholic doctrine that she was 'immaculately conceived', and in the twentieth century Pope Pius XII entitled her 'Queen of Heaven'.

The idea of Jesus as the sacrificial lamb in whose blood sinners may be washed clean may have had its roots in Judaism, but would also have had a great appeal to familiars of the pagan mystery religions which cherished similar ideas. Converts would be likely to endorse and elaborate the concept. Pagan influence probably tended to increase sacerdotalism in Christianity – the ascribing of supernatural powers to priests, religious ceremonies, and consecrated elements. It is interesting to note that, after the destruction of the temple in A.D. 70, Judaism was becoming less sacerdotal as Christianity became more so. Though of minor importance, other indications of pagan influence are to be seen in the fixing of Sunday as the day for worship and 25th December for the celebration of the nativity; both were the dates of pagan festivals.

Despite its absorption of some pagan concepts Christianity was a religion of higher quality than any of its competitors in the Roman Empire. Its belief in a righteous God, its ethical standards, and its principles of love and compassion gave it both moral ascendancy and great appeal. From its origin as a small Jewish sect it spread widely in the Gentile world and, as it spread, tension with the Jews increased to the point of final separation and, eventually, bitter antagonism.

Though Jesus did not create any organisation for the purpose, he clearly expected his disciples to continue his work. For such a purpose he had kept them with him and taught them. In the very early Church there were no formally appointed leaders other than the disciples, now called apostles. It seems that anyone who had the right spiritual gifts was free to take a leading part in his local congregation. Eventually leaders became more formalised and we read of bishops and deacons; but a bishop, in the early days, was not the head of a diocese but merely of a local church.

From the second century onwards, if not earlier, Christianity fragmented into many deviant sects, notably those which came under the general heading of gnosticism. This term derived from the word 'gnosis', i.e. knowledge. This was not factual knowledge but an esoteric spiritual knowledge which was alleged to be the key to salvation. There were strange concepts of higher and lower realms of reality and divinity which had a bizarre effect on ethics: if the essential nature of man, elevated by secret knowledge to a higher sphere, had nothing to do with terrestial life, it mattered not how he behaved in this world.

It was necessary to curb the wilder notions and impose a measure of conformity and discipline on the Christian community. No doubt this strengthened the move towards an authoritative form of leadership, namely sanctified priests and bishops who had much wider authority than they had previously possessed.

During the first three centuries the refusal of committed Christians to offer even a token sacrifice to the pagan gods and the god-emperor of Rome was regarded as a treasonable and unreasonable act. This was deeply resented by some emperors and by many of the people. Consequently Christians suffered sporadic persecution which, under certain emperors, was severe but, under others, persecution virtually ceased. Great courage and steadfastness was shown by many Christians and their faithfulness ensured the spread of their religion throughout the Empire. A considerable proportion of the population was Christian when Constantine became emperor of the Western Empire in A.D. 312 and of the Eastern Empire in A.D. 324. Constantine was not a Christian until he was baptised on his deathbed. He had, apparently, been undisturbed by the previous persecutions and was guilty of some cruel acts, including ordering the murders of his own son and wife. But Constantine was determined to unify the empire and, in pursuance of that objective, he granted religious toleration to all and bestowed rich gifts on the Christians.

Constantine was displeased when he discovered that the Christians themselves were far from being united. There were considerable differences between them both in belief and practice and, at that time, a particularly vicious dispute was raging, known as the Arian controversy. On one side the leading spokesman was Athanasius of Alexandria who asserted the absolute divinity of Christ, claiming that he was the Son of God, of one substance with God, and had existed before the beginning of time. Arius, who led the opposition, was a former pupil of Lucian of Antioch who had stressed the oneness of God, the humanity of Jesus, and the importance of living in accordance with the teaching of Jesus. Arius and his supporters seem to have taken the view that Jesus, though he could be regarded as the Son of God, was not God, equal to God, or one with God; in other words he was a semi-divine figure.

In an attempt to restore unity Constantine, in A.D. 325, summoned Christian leaders from all over the Empire to meet in council in the town of Nicaea. He himself presided, though he knew little Greek and less of Christian theology. The proceedings were acrimonious, but finally Constantine brought pressure to bear in favour of Athanasius and the Alexandrians, so a form of words was agreed which accorded absolute divinity to Jesus. This was later expanded and became the official creed of the Church. It is known as the Nicene creed and includes the words:

We believe in one Lord, Jesus Christ, the only Son of God, eternally begotten of the Father, God from God, Light from Light, true God from true God, begotten not made, one in being with the Father. Through him all things were made. For us men and our salvation he came down from heaven: by the power of the Holy Spirit he was born of the Virgin Mary, and became man. For our sake he was crucified under Pontius Pilate; he suffered, died, and was buried. On the third day he rose again . . . We believe in the Holy Spirit, the Lord, the giver of life who proceeds from the Father and the Son. With the Father and the Son he is worshipped and glorified.

Here is to be found nothing about the love which was such a vital part of the gospel of Jesus. The inspired Galilean prophet has become part of a triune God. God the Father will henceforth have only a share in the worship of men; an even lesser share in later years when adoration of the Virgin Mary became increasingly popular. Christianity had come a long way from Galilee and was to go even further. It seems that some of the delegates at Nicaea signed the formula from fear of Constantine. In his book *Jesus: the Evidence* Ian Wilson writes:

Only on returning home [from Nicaea] did Eusebius of Nicomedia, Maris of Chalcedon, and Theognis of Nicaea summon the courage to express to Constantine in writing how much they regretted having put their signatures to the Nicene formula: 'We committed an impious act, O Prince', wrote Eusebius, 'by subscribing to a blasphemy from fear of you'. But it was too late. Although no Gospel regarded Jesus as God, and not even Paul had done so, the Jewish teacher had been declared Very God through all eternity, and a whole theology would flow from this.

The granting of imperial favour, and the recognition of Christianity as the principal religion of the Empire, had great influence on the administration, government, and ethos of the Church. As it grew in size it had developed a system of deacons, priests, and bishops; and as it became more closely allied to the state so it tended to reflect in its government the autocracy by which Rome ruled. Bishops became men of power and influence governing dioceses. Eventually the Bishop of Rome became absolute head of the Church in the West, though the Greek-speaking Church in the Eastern Empire went its separate way. Later, in medieval Europe, there were prince-bishops who were powerful and wealthy temporal as well as spiritual rulers. In spirit, as in distance, the Church was indeed moving a long way from its origins.

From the fifth century onwards the western Roman Empire declined into economic and social ruin, partly because of its own weakness and internal feuds, partly because of widespread barbarian invasions. War and pestilence attended the collapse of Roman civilisation yet the spread of Christianity continued into the north and west of the continent. The evangelisation was doubtless due, in part, to the work of devoted missionaries, but there was much wholesale 'conversion'. When a pagan chieftain or king decided to embrace the Christian religion, whether for personal or political reasons, his tribe would normally follow. Thus there must have been thousands of nominal Christians who knew little and cared less about the religion to which they had transferred.

The story of Christianity in medieval Europe is a patchwork of good and evil. There were simple, good-living, and dedicated priests like those of the old Celtic Church of Ireland, Iona, and Lindisfarne; monasteries which did much to keep the lamp of learning alight, preserved books, and promoted arts and crafts; and charismatic saints like Francis of Assisi. The Church remained, as it had become in the late days of the Empire, an autocracy ruled by the Pope; sacerdotal, and bound by the creed which was devised at Nicaea, together with the later Athanasian and Apostles creeds. The Church was also corrupted by wealth, power, and nepotism. Superstition was rife and was reflected in the fantastic accounts of miracles and wonders included in the Lives of the Saints which were such popular reading material in medieval days. The crusades were discreditable enterprises being unwarranted attacks by 'Christian' forces on the more cultured and tolerant Arab regime which controlled Palestine. The character of the crusaders was plainly revealed when they sacked the great Christian city of Constantinople. Deviant or reforming movements such as the Cathars and Lollards were persecuted to extinction.

The Reformation of the early sixteenth century was primarily directed against corruption in the Church, but also demanded changes in theology and the sacraments. In the short term the Reformation gave rise to bitter religious wars and much cruel persecution. In the long term it freed Christianity in northern Europe from the autocratic rule of the papacy and led to a greater degree of democracy and freedom of thought in the reformed churches. Though these churches were less sacerdotal than the Roman Church their theology was still based on the historic creeds.

The Church, throughout history, has resisted freedom of thought in respect of any matter which could conceivably affect its orthodox teaching. It therefore opposed, and when it had the power, persecuted deviant thinkers; not only theologians but scientists such as Galileo and Darwin. It is small wonder that Erasmus, one of the great scholars of the Renaissance, was moved to remark that 'to identify the new learning with heresy is to make orthodoxy synonymous with ignorance'. The Protestants, at least until the late nineteenth century, were little better than the Roman Catholics in this respect. Having broken free from an 'infallible' Church and Pope they substituted the authority of an 'infallible' Bible and their interpretation thereof. In his preface to the book entitled *England* Dean Inge wrote:

> Protestantism rightly rejected the infallible Church; it found a poor substitute in the infallible book, a miscellaneous collection of barbarous tribal religion, patriotic pseudo-history, noble religious poetry, sound morality at a rather low temperature, and obscure prophesying attached to the New Testament, which itself contains documents of more than doubtful authenticity. Origen said that if we believed in the literal truth of everything in the Old Testament God was guilty of conduct which would hardly be credited of a human tyrant. . .
>
> When we lament the decay of religion we do not always remember how much we have lost which was not nearly good enough to be true.

The enormous amount of scholarly Biblical research and criticism which took place from the late eighteenth century onwards eventually produced a more liberal attitude, coupled with a greater interest in the historical Jesus and his teaching. However, as evidence accrued that the Gospels were far from being reliable historical records, scholars began to despair of recovering a true picture of the real Jesus. In the book *Concerning Jesus*, edited by D. G. Wigmore-Beddoes, the latter writes:

> The quest of the historic Jesus thus came to a virtual end, and therewith a decline in the popularity of the liberal Protestant interpretation of

Christianity, which laid stress on the religion of Jesus rather than the religion about Jesus, and which saw Christianity more in terms of following Christ rather than in holding correct beliefs about him.

The author goes on to explain that the *kerygma* has become the dominant theme in twentieth-century theology. The *kerygma* being the 'proclamation' of the early Church about the person of Jesus Christ, his death, and resurrection.

Some modern theologians take the view that the origins of Christianity are of little importance compared with what the Church is said to have become – the supreme institution for the saving of men's souls. They claim that the importance of the *kerygma* is not affected by doubts concerning its historical origin.

Other scholars prefer historical facts to myths and present their findings with integrity, but when these would clash with the orthodox creeds they seem reluctant to draw the obvious conclusions. Some will go half way: having come to believe that the divinity of Jesus cannot be supported by an alleged pre-existence, virgin birth, or bodily resurrection, they claim that he was so emptied of self, so filled with the spirit of God, that he may rightly be considered divine. Since nearly all Biblical scholars are in holy orders one can understand their predicament.

Christianity today is not a united but a fragmented religion. There are hundreds of different churches and sects. Though there has been some reunion and a growth in ecumenical feeling, great differences remain. A detached observer might find it difficult to believe that the same religion is professed by a liberal English Free-Churchman and a southern European Roman Catholic; or by a Plymouth Brother and a priest of the Greek Orthodox Church. Between the many churches and sects there are some differences in belief and great differences in emphasis and practice but most, if not all, of them accept the central point of the traditional creeds: the divinity of Jesus. They would probably also agree that salvation is to be found through Christ alone. In church services prayers are addressed to Christ as often as to God, and most prayers are concluded with the words 'through Jesus Christ our Lord. Amen'. God seems to have become a figure in the shadows. Few people have any clear idea what the Holy Spirit is supposed to be, so the only approachable and effective member of the Trinity is Christ. Someone commented with regard to the World Council of Churches that it had become Unitarian – 'of the Son'.

In its long and chequered history the Church (if we may use the term to include all Christian communions) has displayed most of the faults and virtues of which mankind is capable. Though it has often been dogmatic, superstitious, hypocritical, and arrogant, it has also inspired men to works of charity and enlightenment. Even in its darkest hours saintly souls have emerged to recall what Jesus taught concerning the Fatherhood of God and love for our neighbours.

In the twentieth century there has been a dramatic decline in the number of Church members. In the United Kingdom, for example, church attendance has been declining recently at the rate of 50,000 a year and only a small proportion of the population is now closely connected with any church. Many who attend church do so from habit rather than from conviction; for them Christianity is an unexamined faith. They derive some comfort and inspiration from their attendance at church and have no wish to be upset by critical thought. Others doubt the validity of the doctrine and may cease to attend because of their loss of faith. They are unlikely to receive much help in this respect from the sermons, which tend to consist of moral homilies and dogmatic statements unsupported by evidence. Few preachers demonstrate awareness of the findings of Biblical scholarship, or offer reasoned and informed arguments in support of the faith. It is not surprising that one finds many well-meaning folk in the pews but few who are widely read and given to independent thought.

Many individual churches provide a valuable social function as centres for fellowship, youth work, and charitable activities. Above all they uphold good moral standards: a valuable service indeed in an age which has seen a sad decline in such standards.

The creed of the mainstream Christian churches is frozen in a thought-world sixteen centuries old. Their hymns and liturgies express some beliefs and concepts which are unacceptable to thoughtful people today. For many Christians their principal religious activity is attendance at church on Sunday and, in other respects, their way of life differs little from that of their friends and neighbours who do not attend. Sympathy must be extended to ministers who have to preach religion once or twice a week, often to the same congregation. They tend to become stale; congregations become bored and, in Leslie Weatherhead's phrase, 'become so inoculated with religion that they cannot catch it'.

The final point to be made in this brief survey of Christianity is that its claims are absolute and exclusive. If Jesus was God incarnate he must have been unique and right in everything he said and did. John's Gospel reports him as saying 'I am the way, I am the truth, and I am the life; no one comes to the Father except by me'. The *Book of Common Prayer*, after stating the orthodox belief concerning Christ, says 'This is the Catholic Faith, which except a man do faithfully and steadfastly believe, he cannot be saved'. Thus is the vast majority of mankind condemned.

CHAPTER 5

An Assessment

DOES MAINSTREAM CHRISTIANITY, based on the historic creeds, offer a rational and convincing creed for our time? Reference has already been made to the Nicene creed, the first official creed of the Church. The Apostles creed was used in Rome in the third and fourth centuries and reached its final form in France in the early seventh century. It is shorter than the Nicene creed but makes similar affirmations, and both these creeds are recognised and used by most of the churches today. The Athanasian creed is rarely used. Since these creeds are foundation documents of the Christian faith their principal affirmations must be considered.

The creeds commence with an affirmation of belief in God the Father almighty. That, however, is a belief shared by many who are not orthodox Christians. The credal statements which are peculiarly Christian are that Jesus was divine, 'true God from true God', born of a virgin, crucified, and risen from the dead; there is one holy catholic church, one baptism for the forgiveness of sins, resurrection of the body, and life everlasting.

The first point to be noted is that these creeds were devised by fallible men in an age when human knowledge was very limited and when supernatural concepts proliferated. They represent an attempt to reconcile divergent views and explain the inexplicable. As such they deserve our interest, but there is nothing in their origin to command our acceptance and the statements are unsupported by reliable evidence.

The second point to note is that orthodox Christianity is a faith which depends upon miracle. It begins with a miracle, the virgin birth, and ends with the miracle of the resurrection. The doctrine of the Trinity which states that there are three divine persons who comprise one God can only be described as another miracle since it defies logic. All the sound evidence we have indicates that we live in a universe of reliable natural laws. If it be true that the Creator, at times, subverts the order which he himself created we are in deep trouble. No longer can we rely on knowledge or reason, but find ourselves at the mercy of unpredictable magic.

Thirdly, the creeds demonstrate the fact that, from its early days, the Church devoted more attention to the person of Jesus than to his message, which receives no mention.

As suggested in Chapter 3, it is unlikely that Jesus made any claim to divinity. This claim was made by the Church in later years and this deflected Christian theology to such an extent that Dr Paul Trudinger, in his book *Honest to Jesus*, expresses the view that in order to be honest to Jesus it is necessary *not* to be a Christian. It is likely that, to some extent, the miraculous element in the New Testament derived from a felt need to support the claim to divinity. The claim has certainly had a formative influence on Christian practice and theology: for example, the Catholic rite of the mass, and the doctrine of Justification by Faith promulgated by Paul and embraced by Protestants in later years. The classic statement of the latter is found in the Confession of Augsburg, A.D. 1530, which states that men cannot be justified in God's sight by their own merit or works, but only by faith in Christ, who by his own death made satisfaction for their sins. This faith God imputes for righteousness.

It may be, as some affirm, that there is something of the divine in all men and women; but to state that a particular man who lived nearly 2,000 years ago was God incarnate is surely an affirmation which the evidence is quite unable to support. An indispensable piece of evidence would be a complete and absolutely reliable account of his life and, as the previous chapters have indicated, we do not have such a biography of Jesus. It would also be necessary to know that he was without fault in thought, word, and deed; yet such certainty is impossible concerning any man. The records we have of Jesus indicate that, fine man though he was, he probably made some mistakes both of opinion and conduct. His thought-world was also limited by the culture into which he was born. So far as we can tell, no human being is or ever was perfect. If Jesus was perfect he was not human. If he was human he was not perfect. We can, at least, be sure he was human.

Christians are rightly directed to look at Jesus as an example for living. But if he was God incarnate, and sinless, he could not serve as an example to struggling humanity, and it would be useless to say that 'he was tempted in all points as we are, yet without sin'. He could not be so tempted. Our temptations are greatest at points where we have fallen before. A man who has become an alcoholic through previous indulgence finds it infinitely harder to resist a drink than does a man who has been a life-long teetotaler.

We should gladly acknowledge that Jesus was not God but a man and, as such, a fine example to us all. Incomplete and, to some extent, unreliable the Gospel accounts may be; yet they sufficiently portray a man whose spiritual insight and quality of life were superb. Despite considerable misrepresentation, his life and teaching have had great influence in raising the quality of human life and bringing multitudes of people nearer to God. Many who do not accept the creeds respect Jesus and find in him a source of inspiration. Geza Vermes, a Jewish scholar, says of Jesus he was 'second to none in profundity of insight and grandeur of character . . . an unsurpassed master in the art of laying bare the inmost core of spiritual truth and of bringing every issue back to the essence of religion'. But he was not all-knowing, or perfect, and he was not God; nor, apparently, did he claim to be.

The attribution of divinity to Jesus gave rise to a personality cult of such power that, in Christendom, Christ largely replaced God in men's devotion. We have seen, all too vividly in recent years, how dangerous personality cults can be. When we remember the results of the adulation of Hitler and Stalin we may be thankful that Jesus was a good man, and bear in mind that the cult only gathered force after his death. Nevertheless it had some undesirable results. To a considerable degree it locked the beliefs of a great religion in the thought world of the first century. In all other fields of human endeavour progress could take place, but not in Christian doctrine. If Jesus was God, and the records in the Gospels are true, we have already had the ultimate revelation of religious truth and should look for no other. The liturgy, hymns, and lessons used in church tend to perpetuate the ancient beliefs and inhibit any progressive revelation of truth.

A personality cult is nourished by excessive adulation of the subject and, though it is good to admire and praise a fine man, he is not honoured by excess. One aspect of this is the manner in which the Church has tended to glory, one might almost say 'wallow', in the sufferings of Jesus. There is no doubt that he suffered a cruel death, but there is equally no doubt that many thousands of folk have suffered as much or more.

Following the affirmations relating to Jesus the creeds affirm belief in the holy Catholic Church, one baptism for the forgiveness of sins, resurrection of the body, and life everlasting. The Church has always numbered among its members men and women to whom the term 'holy' might properly be accorded, but as an organisation it has never deserved the accolade; and what is meant by 'the Catholic Church'? There are hundreds of different churches, some of which would not acknowledge the right of others to belong to the 'holy Catholic Church'. The 'one baptism for the forgiveness of sins' is an arrogant claim denying, by implication, God's forgiveness to all who fail to undergo a certain rite. It would be difficult to find anyone today who believes in the 'resurrection of the body', though it may be that those who composed the creed did believe it literally. If it is now glossed to mean not 'body' but 'personality' or 'soul' why not say so? Casuistry gives religion a bad name. With regard to belief in the 'life everlasting' it can only be said that there is no reliable evidence for it, so it would be wiser to regard that belief as optional.

In turning to a consideration of the Church two points must first be made. Firstly, for the purpose of this discussion, the word 'Church' signifies those organised Christian communions which are based on the traditional creeds. Secondly, as has been suggested in an earlier chapter, there is no good evidence that Jesus founded, or intended to found, a separate religion or organised body such as the present Christian Church. This was a later creation of other men. In his book *Jesus in Contemporary Historical Research* Gustaf Aulén (Bishop and Professor in Sweden) writes:

The people who gathered round him [i.e. Jesus] were ordinary folk, people of the land, with a small minority of those who were ostracised on social or religious grounds. He created a new community, but it was not his intention to create a new sect; his was an open community with no entrance examinations. Despite the occasional doubtful use of the word *ecclesia* there could have been no question of a 'church' in our sense of the word. Other expressions are more important – the shepherd and the sheep, the new covenant foretold by the prophets, the family who are brothers and sisters. It is evident that Jesus wanted to create a community in anticipation of, and as a foretaste of, the kingdom to come.

The Church came into being after the death of Jesus. Though it had a pious purpose it was not miraculously founded by God but was developed by men, stage by stage, to meet the pressure of events. As an instrument of good religion it has sometimes served well and has sometimes failed. Though the Church has been described as 'Christ's Holy Bride' and believed to be divinely ordained, the fact is that the mission of Jesus might have been continued in other ways and they might even have been better. To sketch even the outline of the long and varied history of the Church is beyond the scope of this small book. The present purpose is simply to consider the 'Faith', the beliefs to which the Church adheres, and to consider whether this constitutes an adequate and sustainable faith for today and for the future.

The view advanced here is that the early Church erred in regarding Jesus as divine and in establishing the faith on alleged miraculous events. These errors were perpetuated by enshrining them in official creeds to which all must adhere who wish to be regarded as Christians. Throughout the Bible and throughout history a widening awareness of God and of his universe has been apparent. Yet the Church has locked itself into beliefs which reflect concepts of the first century. The record is better, though not faultless, with respect to ethical standards. Yet it is sad that a religion which prides itself on sound ethics should display a remarkable indifference to intellectual integrity; an unwillingness to face facts when they appear to contradict 'the Faith'. In *A Free Religious Faith* by Raymond V. Holt, *et al.*, we read the following:

It is sad that the mainstream orthodox churches are still obscurantist and anti-intellectual. For as long as they are able they cling to creeds which were formed long ago in a mental climate which was totally different from that of the twentieth century. The search for truth and the glad acceptance of new revelations in science and historical scholarship ought to be integral to Christian integrity and Christian desire for human progress, but it is rarely found to be so.

For this reason Christianity has lost the allegiance of the majority of intellectually able men and women and . . . is unable to cope with many problems in an enlightened way . . . Because, within the Church, the valuable core of the gospel is linked to and obscured by doctrines of doubtful truth, intelligent people of goodwill are disinclined to become associated with it.

The Christian belief that men and women can only come to God through Christ, and that outside the Church there is no salvation, is bad news for the majority of mankind, both past and present. What is the fate of those who never had the opportunity of knowing about Christ? What of the Hindu and Buddhist saints and seers, the Stoic philosophers, Unitarians and Humanists who have contributed greatly to spiritual life and human betterment? Those who hold such an exclusive creed should consider the possibility that they may be mistaken. In *Jesus: the Unanswered Questions* John Bowden writes:

If traditional Christian doctrine is that God is Trinity, Father, Son, and Holy Spirit, and that God the Son was incarnate in Jesus of Nazareth, it inevitably follows that Christianity is not only different, even from Judaism, but intrinsically by virtue of its official doctrinal position, must claim to be superior . . . Thus Roman Catholics will even now affirm the view of the fifteenth-century Council of Florence that 'no one remaining outside the Catholic Church . . . can become partakers of eternal life', and fundamental evangelicals will have no difficulty with the message of the 1960 Chicago Congress of World Mission, that 'in the days since the war, more than one billion souls have passed into eternity and more than half of these went to the torment of hell fire without even hearing of Jesus Christ, who he was and why he died on the cross of Calvary'.

It is true that many Christian people take a more tolerant and charitable view of those outside the Church but, in so doing, they are moving beyond the tenets of the orthodox faith.

It can be a distressing experience for devout Christians to have doubts concerning the foundations of their faith, particularly when doubt is cast on Jesus Christ as the ultimate truth, the way, and the life. They may ask in anguish 'If we can no longer believe in the reliability of the scriptures, the virgin birth, the incarnation, many of the miracles, and the resurrection, what, if anything, remains?' The short answer is 'There remains what Jesus and the prophets had: God the Father. Rightly understood, that is enough'.

Some liberal Christians accept that parts of the scriptures are historically unreliable and that orthodox doctrines are, to a considerable extent, founded on ancient myths or misconceptions, so they do not accept the doctrines literally but symbolically. This attitude cannot be recommended since it encourages those who are less well informed to continue in unsound beliefs. Also it has an unfortunate effect on intelligent people outside the Church. They do not appreciate the subtle distinction when Christians affirm beliefs, but only symbolically. So they reject Christianity lock, stock, and barrel. In declining to believe in a virgin birth they may 'throw out the baby with the bath water'. Yet the baby became a man whose life and teaching were of such value that, if all knowledge of him were ever to be lost, mankind would be profoundly impoverished.

We find recorded in the Bible the strivings of many good men after truth: truth concerning God, the purpose of life, and how it should be lived. They served their generations well, but they were confined, as all men are, by the limits of the knowledge available to them and were influenced by the culture of the society in which they lived. We shall be nearer to the spirit of these pioneers if we continue the search for truth rather than by regarding their views as final. On some matters we may reach the same conclusions as they did, but the expansion of human knowledge and experience since their time inevitably leads to different conclusions on some matters of importance. Jesus was a radical who challenged many of the customs and orthodoxies of his time and race. But the radical views of the past have a habit of fossilising into the orthodoxies of the present. We might follow Jesus more faithfully by seeking the truth with integrity than by a supine acceptance of ancient orthodoxy.

Despite its errors in creed and practice, the Church has been an influence for good in the world because it has never wholly lost sight of two essential elements of the gospel: the fatherhood of a righteous God and the brotherhood of man. Since these two great principles are at the heart of religion it is sad that the Church has committed itself to some beliefs which are unsound in the light of history and reason: beliefs which fail to convince many thoughtful people today and are likely to seem less convincing as knowledge expands in future years. The finc service rendered by many devoted and warm-hearted members of the Church would be no less valuable and probably more effective if it were based on a rational and convincing faith.

CHAPTER 6

A Path to Faith

Basic concepts are rarely formed by reasoned deductions from the facts. Most are formed in childhood by association; that is to say by the influence of parents, teachers, and other associates. The child's mind is a malleable clay which easily takes impressions which become difficult to change in later life. Religious beliefs which were formed in that way may have to be sustained by regarding religious truth as different from any other. But truth is not divisible and a valid faith must be sustainable in the light of truth from whatever quarter it may come.

It is the purpose of the remaining chapters to suggest that such a faith is possible: one that is tenable on intellectual grounds, receptive of truth from any source, giving a right purpose to life, and cherishing essential values – a faith for living.

It is necessary first to be clear what is meant by 'faith'. For present purposes it may be defined as belief or trust in something or someone when absolute proof of truth or reliability is not available. For example, if a man has been given four apples he can see them, feel them, count them, smell them, and taste them – adequate proof surely that he has four apples. It requires no act of faith to believe that. If the same man has visited a friend and wishes to return home by bus, he may ask his friend's advice and be directed to a certain bus stop where he will be able to catch a no. 20 bus to his own town at 10 p.m. Arriving at the bus stop in good time he checks the timetable displayed there and finds his friend's instruction confirmed. At 10 p.m. a no. 20 bus arrives, displaying the name of his home town as its destination, and he boards it. He has no *proof* that the bus will take him home; the driver may lose his way or run out of petrol. These are very unlikely events, however, and it is highly probable that the man will arrive home. In boarding that bus he has committed an act of faith, but it was a rational act supported by the available evidence. If the man had neither sought guidance nor checked the timetable, but had simply taken the first bus which appeared to be going in the right direction, that would have been an irrational act of faith and, if he arrived at his destination, it would only be by unmerited luck.

Towards the end of his life Bertrand Russell, the philosopher, was interviewed by John Freeman in a television programme. I quote from memory in reporting that Freeman asked 'Have you any advice to offer to those who follow after?' To this Russell replied 'On the intellectual level I would say "look for the facts. Do not look for what you would like to believe, nor even for what you think is socially desirable; but look for the facts, always the facts". On the ethical level I would say "It is clear that human life can only be lived well on this planet if men and women show kindness and consideration one to another. Never forget it".' That advice contains two elements essential to a search for a valid faith: intellectual integrity and sound ethics.

Intellectual integrity implies drawing reasoned and logical conclusions from ascertainable facts and this is an approach to religious faith which many folk would reject. They prefer a faith founded on revelation: God revealing himself to men in the Bible and in the person of Jesus Christ, or in the Koran and through the prophet Mohammed. It must be recognised, however, that any belief requires the use of one's reason. This is necessarily involved in deciding to trust some external authority. The real question is not whether reason should be involved in finding a religious faith, but how it should be employed.

Men are like other animals in that they have instincts, and unlike them because they have the faculty of reason. Frequently there is tension between these two elements in the human psyche; but humans have developed far beyond the stage where instinct suffices and they must depend largely on the use of reason if they are to survive and progress. In this respect they have no choice. This applies as much to religion as to all other aspects of human thought and activity. It is possible to seek an easy security by accepting a faith complete on the authority of a church, a book, or a creed; but that is a hazardous road to take if the credentials of the authority have not been properly examined.

In this world no growth in knowledge or character comes without effort. If we expect to receive a sound faith for living from some external authority, without any effort on our own part, we are looking for a faith 'on the cheap'. We do God more honour by using our minds to learn about him and his world. In religion, as in all other fields of human thought, knowledge is progressive; finality is not to be had in any subject, and certainly not in religion. Those who claim to have it are misguided and can be dangerous. Such people were responsible for religious persecutions in bygone years, and even today they can have a deplorable effect on simple souls who know no better than to accept their 'infallible' dogmas.

Churches which claim final authority, or an infallible gospel usually employ a heightened emotion in their services. This may be by means of an impressive edifice, incense, fine vestments, and music; or, in evangelical sects, by emotional sermons and hymns with congregants singing, clapping, or dancing. Without the warmth of emotion a faith, however true, is likely to be sterile; but excessive emotion, uncontrolled by reason, is more likely to produce religious mania than a sound religious faith. A car without fuel cannot move, and without a driver at the steering wheel it is likely to go in any direction but the right one. If emotion is our motive power, reason is the driver at the wheel.

It goes without saying that a faith should be sincere; but sincerity should extend to examining the truth of the faith as well as the expression of it. It is less than admirable to recite a creed in which one does not believe, and the insincerity is hardly modified by claiming that the words do not mean what they say.

Some religious folk speak of 'having faith' as though that were in itself a virtue. But there is good faith and bad faith; reasonable, examined faith; and unreasonable, unexamined faith. There is certainly no virtue in having the latter. In the book *Together We Advance*, ed. Stephen H. Fritcham, Professor J. L. Adams wrote:

To many people the word [faith] signifies the acceptance of something that puts a strain on the intelligence . . . a belief in what is not true, or is not a fact but a wish. To others the word 'faith' signifies the acceptance of some belief simply because a church, tradition, state, or party demands it.

We have no choice but to be free in the choice of our faith . . . even the man who says he cannot trust his own judgement will have to do so to the extent of deciding what he does trust.

The denial of the right and duty to discuss one's faith is tantamount to making credulity a work of piety . . . the faith that cannot be discussed is a form of tyranny. An unexamined faith is not worth having for it can only be true by accident.

If it be said that the path to a well-founded religious faith may lie through humanism that may be seen as an absurdity or a paradox, depending upon what onc means by 'humanism'. Scholars of the Renaissance, typified by Erasmus, were humanists who did not reject Christianity but moved out of the narrow theological world of their medieval forerunners into a wider sphere of intellectual interest and culture. Much twentieth-century humanism, on the other hand, rejects all religion as an outmoded superstition and is frankly atheist. The term is used here in a sense which lies closer to a dictionary definition; by humanism is meant 'a devotion to human interests, a system concerned with human, as opposed to supernatural matters, with man as a responsible and progressive intellectual being'. To put the matter rather differently, the path to faith must start with what we know, experience, and need. If we have any respect for facts where else can we start?

Religion is immeasurably older than humanism, and we may surmise that it arose from primitive man's awe of phenomena which were beyond his understanding and control: the heavenly bodies, storms, earthquakes, droughts, sickness, and death. These must have seemed to be the work of supernatural powers – gods and goddesses who must be propitiated if one hoped to avoid calamity. The ancient Israelites progressed to a belief in one god who required of men, not only sacrifices, but ethical behaviour.

They also had the story of Adam and Eve who transgressed in the garden of Eden by eating the fruit of the tree of knowledge which God had forbidden them to eat. From this derived the doctrine of original sin, the idea that all human beings are in a state of depravity, from which they can only be redeemed by faith in the atonement wrought by Christ's death upon the cross. As the *Book of Common Prayer* has it 'there is no health in us. But thou, O Lord, have mercy upon us, miserable offenders'.

The idea that all mankind is basically evil is not one that a humanist would accept. He would recognise that the human race has evolved from the animal world beginning, not in original sin, but original ignorance. Mankind has developed self-consciousness, reasoning powers, and a sense of values – the ability to distinguish good from bad, right from wrong. Individual men and women vary greatly in their perception of ethical values and in their response thereto. It may be said that all are sinners in that none live perfectly in accordance with the good they know, but few, if any, are totally depraved. It is morbid and untrue to say 'there is no health in us' since there is some virtue in most people and a great deal in some. Christian doctrine and liturgy have been obsessed by the sin and have tended to ignore the virtue in man.

It is interesting to note that similar views were advanced by Pelagius, a British Christian who lived in the late fourth and early fifth centuries. Pelagius rejected the doctrines of original sin and predestination, asserting that men had free will and an inherent capacity for good. These opinions were vehemently opposed by Augustine and condemned by sundry Church councils. Inevitably Pelagius was excommunicated.

In *The Path of Humanism* Wallace Tavener wrote:

> Humanism is the direction taken by serious thought when it asserts that mankind has a natural disposition and capacity for good. It is seen in its most distinctive form when it comes in conflict with some mode of thought which requires the self-defamation of man. This requirement of self-defamation has obtained a place in orthodox Christian tradition and is especially insisted upon in the 'evangelistic' presentation.

Tavener goes on to say that this is a false antithesis since a kind of humanism has always been an element in religious development.

In the Old Testament we find the worship of God linked with a concern for justice in society, and there is an underlying assumption that men can be expected to appreciate that idea and act upon it. Jesus clearly looked for a similar response to his frequent pleas for a loving concern to be shown to all. This is delightfully illustrated in a number of parables, notably that of the good Samaritan, the story of an act of spontaneous kindness on the part of a man who was, in Jewish eyes, a heretic; but he was humane.

It is sad that the Protestant Reformation did not fully absorb the spirit of the Renaissance with its wider cultural horizons, its enquiring mind, freedom of thought, and intellectual integrity. The reformers tended to substitute for the tyranny of Pope, Church, and dogmas, a new tyranny of Bible, different churches, and different dogmas. Christianity has a long history of opposition to enlightened thinkers.

Social reform in the Western world has, in the main, been effected by men and women who were humane in spirit, whether Christian or not. Rarely has it been the work of organised churches. Clearly it is difficult for churches which are tied to creeds and traditions to initiate radical reforms. These remarks apply, for example, to the abolition of slavery and child labour, the introduction of democracy, and the deliverance of women from their treatment as inferior human beings. The latter reform is still not complete in the Roman Catholic and Anglican Churches and is a classic case of dogma obstructing humane reform. In his book *I Believe in Man* Lord Sorenson wrote:

> In the realm of sex the revolution by non-theological effort has been outstanding. Until recent years the churches did nothing in this vital realm apart from giving negative warnings and exhortations.

He goes on to say, in relation to the use of contraception devices to control unwanted pregnancies and population explosion:

> The Christian Church can take no credit whatever for this human boon which yesterday it condemned as inimical to holy matrimony, purity, and divine law.

It is self-evident that a good faith for living must have a deep concern for the welfare of our race, and the term 'welfare' includes spiritual and aesthetic as well as material values. There is a sense in which this concern must be intellectual, for we often face social problems of great complexity which can only be solved by intelligent study of the facts, unhampered by ancient prejudice or dogma. It must also be a warm concern for individuals issuing in personal acts of kindness. It has been said of Rousseau that 'he combined a love of all mankind in general with a hatred of all mankind in particular'. Therein is a salutary warning. Heart and mind must both be involved in a humane faith, and we must never become so obsessed by the mob that we cannot see the men and women.

Humanism, in the sense in which it is here commended, is not an esoteric philosophy, still less an atheistic creed, but an affirmation that mankind has an inherent capacity for good. Many who can properly be called humanists also cherish the belief that God has made men so. This view of life involves a realistic awareness of the many evils in the world, an eagerness for reform, and a belief that, if men and women dedicate their lives and service to that end, the reforms will surely come. Prime evidence for the validity of such a view is not to be found in any theory, philosophy, or theology, but in our normal experience of the spontaneous kindness of ordinary people. When a person suffers a serious affliction of illness or bereavement the response of friends and neighbours in offering help and comfort is remarkable, and is by no means confined to those who are overtly religious.

Despite many serious setbacks the main trend of human history has been progressive. A good faith for living must be both realistic and optimistic. As Arthur Hugh Clough wrote:

> For while the tired waves vainly breaking,
> Seem here no painful inch to gain,
> Far back, through creeks and inlets making,
> Comes silent, flooding in, the main.

To quote again from Wallace Tavener's *The Path of Humanism*:

Those who content themselves with lamentations over evil obscure the fact that the perception of evil in the world is proof of the will to good in ourselves . . . A humanist is one who, knowing evils, and in spite of them, thinks constructively and hopefully of mankind. He holds that men and women should be encouraged to bestir themselves, not knowing how much good can be achieved until it is wholeheartedly attempted. . . . Though a philosophy of the worst may be possible, he claims that a philosophy of the best is equally possible and more purposeful; and is certain that no philosophy can be adequate that does not take knowledge of the best as well as the worst.

CHAPTER 7

A Faith for Living

PHILOSOPHERS AND THEOLOGIANS have offered arguments for a belief in God which were often more recondite than convincing, bringing to mind the familiar jingle:

> Forasmuch as without Thee
> We are not able to doubt Thee,
> O grant us Thy grace
> To inform the whole race
> We know nothing whatever about Thee.

The fact is we have no hard evidence to prove the existence of God. However, the fact that *proof* is not available does not preclude the possibility of a reasonable *faith* that God does exist; a faith consistent with the known facts. It should be noted that the atheist who denies the existence of God is making a leap of faith similar to that of the religious man who affirms it. The former is no more able than the latter to offer conclusive proof of his belief.

There are many areas of human thought, other than religion, wherein there is no possibility of scientific proof: philosophy, aesthetic appreciation of art, literature, and music; political and legal opinions – to name but a few. Nevertheless, choices have to be made, and a careful, fair, and logical consideration of the available evidence can lead to conclusions which are generally regarded as valid. We should look for proof where that is available, and when it is not we should look for the highest degree of probability in the light of reason and the available evidence.

In considering what power, if any, created the universe we can only start with the fact of the universe itself. Scientists offer plausible theories as to how the universe in general, and our planet in particular, developed; but how did it all begin? A widely accepted theory at the present time is known as the 'hot Big Bang'. This describes the universe originating from a tiny mass of infinite density, called a 'singularity', which exploded or expanded with incredible force somewhere about 15 billion years ago. Apparently the scientific model, though it can describe the expansion, cannot account for the singularity. There are other theories which have a bearing on this but no scientist, thus far, seems able to offer a theory which accounts satisfactorily for all the phenomena. What is clear, however, is that only a very remarkable balance of forces made it possible for the universe to reach its present state and, in particular, for planet Earth to become habitable by an intelligent race.

In his article 'The Relationship between Faith and Reason', *Faith and Freedom*, vol. 45 (1992), Professor Paul Badham wrote:

> In recent years belief in an eternal creator has become more reasonable as there appears to be a growing consensus that the universe has not always existed . . . If this is true then the universe is not self-explanatory, and any explanation has to postulate some reality transcendent to it. Other scholars are impressed by signs of apparent design in the way the universe has evolved, and interpret the so-called 'anthropic principle' as suggesting that a mind not wholly without analogy to our own lies behind it.

The fact that the universe, our planet, and *homo sapiens* evolved through the operation of what we call 'natural laws' does not necessarily postulate an inchoate force as the origin, nor does it preclude the possibility of an intelligent and purposeful creator. It might be fair to ask who or what established the natural laws. If a craftsman designed and made a certain artefact by hand none would deny that he had created it. If the man had the necessary skill and resources, he might use a computer to design the artefact and employ automated machinery to produce it in large numbers, but he is surely still the creator. 'Natural laws' may be the method employed by the creator to achieve the results he desires.

Scientists are able to tell us a great deal about the mechanics, the natural laws, which operate in the universe to produce the results we observe. They can tell us 'how', but seem to be in no better position than the theologians to pontificate on the answer to the question 'who or what is the ultimate creative power?'

In his book *Reality* Professor B. H. Streeter pointed out that, in coming to a valid opinion about most things, we need to consider values as well as statistics. Thus, in order to have a proper opinion of a city such as Venice, it is necessary to have regard to its beauty and culture as well as its size, population, and wealth. It is easy to be so overwhelmed by fantastic astronomical statistics that we forget to look for values in the universe; a universe in which our planet is statistically insignificant. Yet on this little Earth an extraordinary set of circumstances has given rise to a race of intelligent beings which has already acquired a vast corpus of knowledge and a sense of moral, aesthetic, and spiritual values. It seems there is more to this universe than statistics; for how can mathematics, physics, and chemistry account for love, goodness, truth, and beauty?

If, lacking direct evidence, we look for a rational faith concerning the ultimate creative and controlling power of this marvellous universe we probably have to choose between the conceptions of a blind force and an infinite, intelligent, and purposeful being. It is suggested that the latter conception accounts better for the phenomena than does the first.

If that proposition be accepted it may be regarded as a foundation for a reasonable faith and we may build on it. In *Reality* Streeter also stated, with regard to living creatures, that the higher they are in the scale from the most primitive to the most highly developed, the more apparent become such qualities as individuality and the capacity for independent action. One could hardly regard an amoeba as having an individual personality, but this quality becomes more apparent in higher forms of life and is found fully developed in the human species. If that which created the universe were an inchoate force it would be inferior to many of its creations; which is unlikely. It is reasonable to suppose, therefore, that the creator has all the qualities of the highest known form of life, personality and character, and much more also.

It is, therefore, not inappropriate to use the word 'God' for the creative power. Certainly this is an anthropomorphism and, by definition, a limited representation. Yet it is a useful one since our finite minds are incapable of comprehending the infinite. If we have never seen, and cannot expect to see, Mount Everest, we would be able to visualise it to a limited extent if we were to be shown a fine painting of the mountain. The picture would be only a small object of paint and canvas and could not compare in size and grandeur with the mountain itself. Nevertheless it would help us to have a valid conception of the greatest mountain on Earth. The belief in a personal God which is common to the Semitic religions: Judaism, Christianity, and Islam, is a conception of great value but we must remember that, like the picture of Everest, it has limitations. Asian religions may remind us of this fact. In *Christianity in the Light of the East* (Hibbert Lecture 1987) Bede Griffiths said:

> Hinduism, though it allows for a creator God, prefers to speak of Brahman, the infinite, eternal reality beyond word and thought, which is the origin and end of the universe. Perhaps the essential difference between the two outlooks is that for the Semitic religions God is essentially transcendent, separate from the world, while in the Asian religions, God, or the first principle of being, is essentially immanent. It is the 'ground' of being, the inner reality which sustains the whole creation . . . it is not pantheism, by which is meant that all is God, but pan-en-theism, which means that God is in all things.

If God, then, exists and is the ultimate creative power, eternal, omniscient, and omnipresent, the question arises as to whether he is moral, amoral, or immoral. If the question seems foolish we must reflect that many of the gods conceived by men in ancient times were anything but moral. It seems reasonable to make deductions concerning the creator from what we know of his creations. Concerning moral values the only creatures which appear to have relevance are human beings since they alone are rational and capable of moral judgements. If we see a beautiful picture we may rightly surmise that the artist had a sense of beauty. If we see a man, at considerable cost to himself, give succour to a person in distress we may assume that the man is kind and compassionate.

The objection may be made that this line of thought can lead to no clear conclusion since, in this world, evil things are done as well as good. The evil, however, seems to arise from primitive instincts which men have not outgrown or controlled, or which have been perverted. The good seems to arise from a different and unique spirit in man. Goodness, truth, justice, and kindness are widely admired and valued. Cruelty and many other forms of evil are abhorred. This has been so throughout historical times and it is significant that moral standards have steadily risen. The fact that there have been serious setbacks must not be allowed to obscure the fact that the long-term picture is one of progress. Mankind's appreciation of what is good, and progress towards it, surely tells us something important about the nature and purpose of the Creator.

An apparent obstacle to belief in a good and loving God is presented by the evil and undeserved suffering in the world. Some attribute this to a malevolent spirit, variously named the Devil, Satan, or Beelzebub; an unconvincing explanation, not least because there is clearly no need for it. A good God can be presumed to have a good purpose for mankind; but men can only grow in character if they have freewill, and that involves risks. It is impossible to have one without the other. We have to learn to choose between good and evil, to cope with misfortune as well as good fortune. Most of the evil and suffering arise from the failure of men and women to use their faculties to good purpose. There is no need to invent an imaginary devil to take the blame. If all the skill, courage, and endeavour that have gone into aggressive and selfish pursuits had been devoted to good government, medical work, the pursuit of knowledge, and looking after the needy, the evil and suffering would have been dramatically reduced. Even the suffering resulting from natural disasters would have been minimised if people had used the intelligence God gave them; for example, by not building their homes in areas known to be subject to floods or earthquakes.

If men and women had been so made that they could only behave well they would be mere automatons. If appropriate punishment or reward followed every act there would be no undeserved suffering, but the world would be like a gigantic slot-machine in which everybody got exactly what they paid for. There would be no scope for love, charity, or self-sacrificial service and, therefore, no character development. That sort of world would not be worth living in. Suffering is hard to bear, but it is an inevitable concomitant of free will, and it is our high calling to use the latter to reduce the former.

If God has established a natural order in which men and women can grow in character it is not reasonable to expect him to intervene by performing miracles. If God were to intervene occasionally to save people from catastrophe by supernatural means that would be unfair to those not so saved. If he were to intervene on all occasions when folk were under threat the natural order would be reduced to chaos and the cure would be worse than the disease. Rational faith does not expect God to work by magic but gratefully accepts that he is revealed in the orderly universe and in the mind of man. It also accepts that we can never have a complete knowledge of God, so an honest theology must be diffident and recognise that dogmatic certainty is inappropriate.

There must also be an awareness that modern science is not omniscient and there is a great deal yet to learn. The human race is young and has a long way to travel. A pamphlet published by the Greenpeace organisation, having reminded us that our planet is about 4,600 million years old, went on to say that if this time-span be reduced to an understandable concept of 46 years, we can say that only at age 42 did the Earth begin to flower. Mammals arrived eight months ago. In the middle of last week ape-like men appeared, and modern man has been around for four hours. He discovered agriculture in the last hour and the industrial revolution began a minute ago. On such a time scale who can predict the future discoveries of the human race? With G. K. Chesterton we may say:

> For there is good news yet to hear and fine things to be seen
> Before we go to Paradise by way of Kensal Green.

It therefore behoves science, like theology, to observe a decent diffidence and admit the limitations of its knowledge. Two small examples are an indication of this: dowsing and telepathy. Though the evidence is inconclusive, the success rate appears to exceed what could be expected from coincidence and science cannot account for the phenomena. We have a great deal to learn about the natural world and about how God works through it. Perhaps spiritual and material realities are not the dichotomy we imagine them to be.

Many people feel the need for a more intimate contact with God than that which has so far been discussed. Is it possible and do any folk experience it? What are we to make of the claims of those who say they have had mystical experiences – hearing voices, seeing visions, or simply a consciousness of the presence of God? Such experiences are subjective and cannot be directly tested. In Bernard Shaw's *Saint Joan* when Robert de Baudricourt questions Joan she tells him 'I hear voices telling me what to do. They come from God'. Robert tells her that they come from her imagination. To which Joan replies 'Of course. That is how the messages of God come to us'. A claim to a mystical experience can only be tested by judging the integrity and mental stability of the person making the claim, and the quality of the experience they have had or the message they have received. Some claims pass the test and some do not.

The Oxford Group, in the 1930s, made a great point of holding 'quiet times' to seek 'guidance'. Many folk who came into the Group had no background of intelligent religious thought. The result was that the 'guidance' they claimed to have received was frequently bizarre, infantile, or frivolous. During the period when the Group flourished someone asked a distinguished Quaker scholar whether he believed in guidance. He replied 'Yes, but not for boys'. That reply may appear to be supercilious but it makes a useful point. The rewards of prayer are not to be had cheaply but are likely to be fruitful in proportion to the sincerity, thought, and experience which folk bring to it. There are probably many who believe they have experienced God, not in any dramatic vision or voices, but in a sense of a quiet and reassuring presence and an enlightening of the mind. They deserve to be taken seriously. Indeed it is very probable that God speaks to us and touches us in the ordinary way of life and through our human contacts. Dr Leslie Weatherhead once recounted the story of a minister who was called to the house of a young woman tragically bereaved of her husband. When the minister entered the room a woman friend was holding the widow in her arms, comforting her. The girl turned to the minister and said bitterly 'Where is your God now?' There flashed through the minister's mind a line of verse 'But hush, I pray you, what if that friend happen to be God?'

A widely held faith which lies clearly beyond our knowledge and experience is the Christian 'sure and certain hope of the resurrection to eternal life'. A hope it may be; sure and certain it is not, since it lacks any reliable supporting evidence. A very thorough investigator, who was known to me, spent years examining phenomena allegedly coming from beyond the grave. He came to the conclusion that the majority of the claims were fraudulent and the remainder resulted from delusion. He found none that was genuine. It is a fact of the natural world that all living things die, and they also reproduce. They leave behind them younger trees, animals, birds, and fish similar to, but not identical with, the parents. Thus there is continuity of life, but not of the life of the individual. We have no evidence that human beings are unique in that the personality survives when body and brain are dead.

Do we really want to live for ever? If the matter is carefully considered there are many who will find the prospect unattractive. There are some strange ideas about how eternity might be spent. For example, a familiar hymn has the word 'What rapture will it be, prostrate before Thy throne to lie and ever gaze on Thee!' People who live to a great age often show little interest in eternal life. They are very tired and wish only to fall peacefully into sleep and never wake.

The traditional hope for eternal life unfortunately diverts attention from an important aspect of survival: the surviving *influence* of personality. This is particularly potent in the relationship between parent and child and may also be strong in other relationships. Anyone who has experience of deep psycho-analysis knows how powerful this influence can be. Throughout our lives we are all making our influence felt on other people, for good or ill; leaving, as it were, something of ourselves in them. The process is continuous from generation to generation – a sobering thought which should cause us to mend our ways. This is not strictly immortality, but it is a process which will continue as long as the human race exists. There is also a form of survival in the memory of those who are left behind, and it can be very precious. So William Cory could write of a departed friend:

> Still are thy pleasant voices, thy nightingales, awake;
> For death, he taketh all away, but them he cannot take.

We should recognise the limits of our knowledge of ultimate things, and try to leave behind us an influence for good which will survive in those we know and be transmitted by them to their children.

It may always be beyond the capacity of the human mind to comprehend ultimate reality. In that excellent, though now defunct, journal *The British Weekly* Dr J. A. Hutton once wrote 'The sun in the heavens is a gift by which we see our way, not something to be gazed at until, blinded by the blaze, we turn our eyes on this world and see – nothing'. The light we have is ample for our needs. That light becomes brighter and horizons widen as the human race progresses, yet there will always be mysteries beyond.

Religious faith is not, and cannot be, an exact science. It is, therefore, foolish to attempt to confine it in a strait-jacket of fixed dogma or creed. This could only be justified if God had revealed himself to man completely and finally; but this is clearly not so. The revelation is continuous in widening knowledge and in increasing awareness of, and sensitivity to, moral issues. The invaluable revelation of God which we find in the Bible and in the person of Jesus has been and will be widened and illumined by generations of those who seek truth and goodness. In *A Free Religious Faith*, Raymond V. Holt, *et al.*, we read:

The historic religions were, to a large degree, products of the cultures out of which they emerged. When they emerged there was no effective, or very limited, communication between one culture and another, no world-wide corpus of knowledge or view of life. Each of these religions was, therefore, limited both in its basic knowledge and in its views. The modern world is very different: the bounds of human knowledge have widened immensely and its dissemination is world-wide. In this situation a religion which is bound to a particular culture which existed centuries ago cannot expect to be either credible or effective.

An adequate faith for living today must cherish the spiritual insights bequeathed from the past but readily accept new revelations of the truth no matter whence they come. It has to be a free religious faith in the sense of recognising the wide variety of spiritual insights in individual men and women. Probably no two people have precisely similar views on matters of religious faith. Tolerance and sympathy are essential and should extend to members of non-Christian faiths. We should be willing to share with them and learn from them, abandoning arrogant ideas such as 'outside the Church there is no salvation'.

Those who are within the Judaeo-Christian tradition have spiritual insights to share with those of other faiths, but the others have something to share with them. We may take for an example the great Hindu poet and mystic, Rabindranath Tagore. The following extracts are from his *Gitanjali and Fruit Gathering*.

My poet's vanity dies in shame before thy sight.
O master poet, I have sat down at thy feet.
Only let me make my life simple and straight,
like a flute of reed for thee to fill with music.

Here is thy footstool and there rest thy feet
where live the poorest, and lowliest, and lost.
When I try to bow to thee my obeisance cannot reach
down to the depth where thy feet rest
among the poorest and lowliest and lost.
My heart can never find its way to where
thou keepest company with the companionless
among the poorest, the lowliest, and the lost.

This is my prayer to thee, my lord –
strike, strike at the root of penury in my heart.
Give me the strength lightly to bear my joys and sorrows.
Give me the strength to make my love fruitful in service.
Give me the strength to raise my mind high above
daily trifles.
And give me the strength to surrender my strength
to thy will with love.

Who will say that we have nothing to learn from a man who writes such words? It is common practice in Unitarian Free Churches to read, as lessons, passages such as these, as well as passages from the Bible; and a very admirable practice it is.

In the Introduction it was suggested that there is a great need today for a rational faith which would give a right purpose to life. But is that true? Many people seem to go through life fairly happily without being conscious of any such need. They appear to be satisfied with the normal round of home life, work, and leisure pursuits; have little concern for social problems, and are only aroused by threats to their own immediate interests. Against that picture of modest domestic bliss another must be shown to illustrate the urgent need for help and reform in the human society of which we are all a part. The scourge of war has been terrible in this century and is far from being eliminated. The two world wars caused unprecedented destruction of human life and property and a United Nations Association official has stated that, since the Second World War, there have been 200 further wars with 16 million people killed and 12 million refugees. In what is known as 'the Third World' famine and abject poverty are widespread and medical services desperately scarce. The more prosperous countries are plagued by a rising crime rate, drug addiction, and sexually-transmitted disease; and many people, in various parts of the world, do not enjoy basic human rights. The catalogue of wrongs is endless and these will only be righted by the efforts of men and women who believe they have a responsibility to serve and have that as a purpose in life. This is where reform must begin: in a faith for living. As the late Dr T. R. Glover said 'You can do nothing with men until you change their master thought'.

It was stated above that the path to a sound faith can lie through humanism. Since humanism is an interest in and a concern for the welfare of humanity, it follows that the faith must be an ethical faith devoted to that welfare. Such an approach also implies that we start from the facts we know – our world and our human race – to seek a knowledge and awareness of the Creator. In these endeavours intellectual integrity is essential. We must gladly receive any revelation of the truth, being ready to learn from both the past and the present unhampered by ancient dogmas. If the faith is to be a faith for living, and not just a theory, it must be expressed in our daily work and voluntary service; in politics, education, social work, or simply in helping the family and neighbours. It matters not how obscure the service may be. Fame is not always the spur and much good is done by those who seek no credit for it.

Such a faith claims that human life has meaning and purpose; that each generation should bequeath to posterity deeper and wider truths than it inherited and should create a better quality of life for people the world over. Those comments apply to the whole range of human activity, not just to the specifically religious. The old ideals of goodness, truth, and beauty are to be cherished. There is no harm in having our heads in the air if our feet stay on the ground. It helps to remember that good sense is a sense of proportion fortified by a sense of humour.

Both active Christians and those who are outside the Church may wonder whether a free religious faith can have any use for the practice of meeting for fellowship and worship. Certainly it can. Possibly in the Society of Friends, and certainly in the Unitarian Free Churches, the views here expressed would meet with a wide measure of agreement; and these people meet for fellowship and worship. Indeed Unitarian scholars and preachers have been expressing similar views for a long time. It is sad that their numbers are few and their views have not been widely known. They have found it hard to make an impression on the established beliefs. Once a religion has become firmly established in a community it tends to be self-perpetuating despite any invalidity of its dogmas.

A good church service provides inspiration, edification, and the opportunity to worship in fellowship. But many who attend the mainstream Christian churches have doubts concerning the traditional beliefs. This can give rise to withdrawal symptoms and a feeling of hypocrisy. A free religious faith does not demand adherence to any creed, recognising that theology must be diffident and progressive, that each person has an individual view of God and ultimate realities. A church which recognises these facts offers a welcome to all without preconditions. Those who cannot accept the traditional creeds and join a church where there is freedom and integrity of thought experience a lightening of the heart. At last they feel able to worship in spirit and in truth. Such a faith can have sympathetic and fruitful contacts with members of other faiths, and might well, eventually, be seen to have universal appeal.

This faith for living is simple, radical, and dynamic. Though the full nature of God is beyond our comprehension, for our human purposes we can rightly think of him as a righteous, loving, and eternal Father. We can turn to him just as we are and find acceptance. The only condition is that we sincerely desire to seek his truth and do his will by caring for our fellow men and women. This message was given by Jesus and is supported by many other inspired teachers. To myths, creeds, sacraments, and conventional observances we can be totally uncommitted. This is a religion, to use Dr Nathaniel Micklem's words 'which faces reality, needs no external credentials, is not a system of dogmas, nor a mysterious experience, but the right attitude to life'. That right attitude to life must surely include gratitude and devotion to the Creator who has given that life. This may be expressed in thought, prayer, and worship; but primarily in our quality of life. We honour God most by helping others. If faith is for living, worship is in the way we live.

Such a faith may be welcomed by intellectuals because it rejects obscurantism and seeks truth; yet it is basically simple and brings to mind an aphorism of the late Sir Arthur Quiller-Couch: 'The highest universal truth is a thing so simple that a child may understand it'. This is not a faith which would bring a crowd in

Wembley Stadium to a pitch of emotional fervour. It may, however, have a strong appeal to those who think.

Some lines by George Russell, though written in a different context, are also relevant in the context of this theme:

> The generations as they rise
> May live the life men lived before,
> Still hold the thought once held as wise,
> Go in and out by the same door.
> We leave the easy peace it brings:
> The few we are shall still unite
> In fealty to unseen kings
> Or unimaginable light . . .
> No blazoned banner we unfold –
> One charge alone we give to youth:
> Against the sceptred myth to hold
> The golden heresy of truth.

Short List for Further Reading

Aulén, Gustaf, *Jesus in Contemporary Historical Research* (London, 1976)

Bowden, John, *Jesus: The Unanswered Questions* (London, 1988)

Brown, Colin, *Philosophy and the Christian Faith* (Illinois, 1968)

Butterfield, H., *Christianity and History* (London, 1949)

—— *Christianity in European History* (London, 1952)

Price, E. Shirvell, ed. *Adventures in Religion* (London, 1968)

Rowland, Christopher, *Christian Origins* (London, 1985)

Tavener, Wallace, *The Path of Humanism* (London, 1968)

Wilson, Ian, *Jesus: The Evidence* (London, 1984)